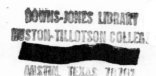

W9-BCE-344

tennis anyStyle,

scientifically

by John D. Borsos

"First Edition"

Third Level Books

Matawan, New Jersey

Copyright © 1990 by John D. Borsos

First Printing 1990

Library of Congress Catalog Card Number: 89-90566

International Standard Book Number: 0-9624182-3-4

Printed in the United States of America

84813

Contents

the problems of learning

Tennis has a number of attractive features and interesting attributes, among them the feel of rhythm and power that comes with a well executed stroke, the exhilaration of competition, the satisfactions of solid hits, the priority of technique over strength, the suitability for all age groups and all types of physiques, and even the high level of difficulty that imparts an aura of artistry and achievement to those who are proficient.

There are few sports where size has as little importance. One drawback is that to be good at it requires spending a lot of time, regularly. But during that time a person obtains not only the satisfactions mentioned but also a quota and level of exercise that everyone needs and that cannot be delegated.

GETTING STARTED

Good tennis strokes are not a matter of natural talent but acquired skills. A person need not be exceptional in either physique or athletic ability to become an accomplished tennis player. But it is not possible to learn to play an effective game of tennis without getting

1

some type of instruction: either by taking lessons from a coach, watching instructional film, watching good players in action, reading books on tennis, or a combination of these.

Those players who are not able to base their games on some such foundation are almost certain to develop makeshift styles with limited potential. The strokes of poor players range from atrocious idiosyncrasies to ostensibly correct patterns that are nevertheless highly artificial in execution. An athletically built young man with wrong tennis habits may not be able to hit much more than ineffective push or slap shots, while a thin little girl may be able to hit deep and powerful drives.

THE DIFFICULTY OF INTRODUCING CHANGES

Once a person's techniques become habit through numerous repetitions then it seems that for almost everybody no amount of practice or traditional instruction can make any real change in the basic stroke patterns. If this were not true, so that top physique and talent, top instruction, and unlimited practice were sufficient to revise any technique however well ingrained, then it could be expected that all tournament players would have almost identical unreturnable first serves.

Players fall into categories as determined by the types of games they play. And it seems that improvement has been possible only within categories, leaving many devotees of the game perpetually confined by an initial unfortunate choice of technique to corresponding levels of mediocrity and ineptitude. In other words, it has not been possible to become a player of a different type, only a slightly better or much worse player of the same type. It is an aim of this book both to remove the limitations on progressive advancement from level to level and to forestall the common and constant drift toward deterioration.

The rationalization that instructors often use in regard to a consistent failure to change mediocre or worse games to the game of anyone's dreams is that once students have taken a series of suitable lessons then it is their own inflexibility and lack of talent that prevent then from mastering the techniques that were described, demonstrated, and practiced during the lessons.

This excuse may have validity in some cases. However the experts themselves are bound by similar restrictions, albeit at a higher level, and have little or no more success with rebuilding their own games than the dubs do with theirs. It is necessary to uncover the ties that bind all levels of players to techniques and results that they themselves may detest, and to develop the means, if any, by which those ties can be broken.

CONFORMITY TO STYLE

At one time it was claimed that the single correct style for all players was the classic. But the belief that excellence was synonymous with conformance was probably more the result of a desire to simplify and codify the teaching methods than to emulate the successful techniques used by the top stars. Observation of such players shows that there is a great deal of variation in grip, stance, attitude of racquet, end point of swing, position of feet, use of wrist, etc.

An oft used rationalization of this variation is that because of their exceptional talent the pros can get away with unorthodox methods that would not be at all suitable for lesser players. This excuse neglects the fact that the athletically gifted players are apt to have a knack for recognizing what is and what is not effective regardless of the degree of conformity to theory or tradition. They are skilled at being able to learn from each experience and to discard or modify whatever they find to be ineffective, even if those things are held to be sacred dogmas.

While many of the mannerisms of less talented players are well known atrocities it is nevertheless unfair to require those fans to conform blindly to what may be just elementary orthodoxy, and thus in cases actually deny them advantages that help the experts attain their superior level of play. Coaches now generally agree that it can no longer be assumed that all students must learn to do the same things the same way, even though a diversity of styles adds greatly to the teaching problems.

BAD HABITS

Although improvements are hard to come by it is evident that bad habits attributable to wrong ideas, emotional reactions, gratification of urges, lazy execution, etc., and whether intended to compensate for imagined insufficiencies at one extreme or to overwhelm the ball with greater than human power at the other, are acquired all too easily and imperceptibly but soon become fixed all too permanently, and usually well before there is any awareness of their existence.

The anomaly of the difficulty of learning a good habit compared with the great ease in acquiring a bad can be partly explained by the fact that the desired good habits are just observed external events, while the wrong habits have internal origins. Many of the wrong techniques are often more or less automatic adjustments introduced to make up for more basic flaws, or for one's own presumed athletic limitations and inadequate early training.

While it is technique that delivers the ball it is habit that largely controls technique. Since it is true that repetition is instrumental in creating habit it is easy to assume, despite almost total evidence to the contrary, that the same type of repetition can also change habit. But although new strokes can be fairly easily acquired, such as the double-handed shot as a replacement for the single, almost all attempts at the more important and more frequent task of inserting desired corrections into existing techniques have been marked by frustrating failure.

Explanations and analysis, demonstrations, emulation of complete patterns, breaking strokes down into components, use of video replay, etc., have neither individually nor in combination been very effective in redesigning flawed styles. This makes it appear that habit developed through an initial series of repetitions cannot be totally replaced by habit expected to emerge from a subsequent series of repetitions.

THE INTERNAL CONTROLS

Most player's strokes are controlled by a set of ideas, impulses, habits, and expectations that take over at the start of every stroke, rather than that they are controlled by conscious intentions or by what might be expected to be learned from the appreciations and agonies experienced during and after countless previous strokes.

Some controlling internal factors can be readily identified: emotions, motives, gratifications, laziness, lack of confidence, misinformation, fanciful expectations, etc. They will be analyzed and discussed in detail later, together with how some can be used to enhance rather than prevent new learning. If the control exercised before a stroke by unreal expectations can be superseded at least in part by that derived from the appreciations of good techniques as experienced during execution, then the major roadblocks to replacing bad habits can be removed.

Some elements that exert control over the way that a person hits derive that influence partly just because of having priority in time, not because of considerations of importance or rationality. In this respect anticipations can assume undue importance because they come first, while appreciations derived from the manner of execution are ignored simply because they come last, when regret is one of the few remaining options. Mere repetitive practice is not very helpful because the new techniques are not likely to originate out of any internal urges and are not inherently a source of much appreciation.

REPETITION RATIOS

There also is a problem of how to promote carry-over from practice into play, especially since most players are unwilling to risk new techniques during a game, even those that are merely social. Consequently the old methods are generally being used several times or even as much as hundreds of times as often as the new, and the old are thereby unwittingly being proportionately reinforced rather than progressively replaced.

In that event the desultory attempts to master new techniques often become nothing more than a source of confusion. The knowledge of the effect of repetition on retaining the bad instead of learning the good may in itself be useful in inducing some players to change the repetition ratio in favor of the good habits, and thus increase the chances of new ideas being assimilated.

PROBLEMS WITH CHOICES

Even if repetition could change habit it is not at all certain that a particular technique or style being considered as a replacement, however classic and elegant or simple and rational, is really any better if the old happens to be quite effective though not exactly pretty. In choosing new techniques there is always the danger of lesser results and satisfactions in spite of improved appearance. In order to be able to continually adjust one's game in the light of experience it is necessary to develop at least some ability to recognize when the supposedly desirable is actually so, as well as when the supposedly bad is not bad in fact.

Since not everything is known, and even some "known" things are wrong, it is a wise player who can correctly decide which recommendations to listen to and which to ignore. There have been cases when even top tournament players with the best coaches made changes that turned out to have very negative consequences. An aim of this book is to develop sufficient guidelines so that such misfortunes are unlikely to occur even to ordinary level players and coaches.

THE TASK AHEAD

In order to help make such discrimination possible a considerable examination of proper and improper influences and hitting techniques will be presented. The relevant principles of hitting, whose violation tends to be the trademark of the dub and whose observance that of the skilled tennis player, will be extensively examined.

The intent is to relate the problems that students have to the violation of related physical laws, and to base learning not on stroke patterns but on the satisfactions ensuing from the observance of the rules that optimize the processes basic to any stroke regardless of style. It is also necessary to be able to consciously recognize the unpleasantness that goes with doing things in a wrong way before the subconscious and the muscles can be persuaded to prefer the obviously more desirable techniques.

A problem for both teachers and students is that the factors of a stroke are so interrelated that it may seem necessary to talk about everything all at once. An absolutely correct suggestion from the teacher may not have a positive effect for the student because the execution is dependant on a knowledge of other actions that novices are not apt to be familiar with. While it may be entirely impractical for the teacher to go through all the intricacies of a stroke it is somewhat of an impediment to success not to.

In an attempt to get at least a partial solution to this problem the sequence of topics in this book depends on the relatedness of concepts rather than on an orderly description of techniques. It is the principles of hitting that are being developed rather than the standard patterns and the "how-to" directions that go with them. Such directions are not the province of this book since the concepts being presented are intended to apply to any tennis stroke in any style.

chapter two
elasticity

It is obvious that the only part of a swing that has any direct effect on the ball is the interval of contact of racquet and ball. Standard formal instruction covers such other elements as grip, footwork, stance, preparation, swing, and follow-through in rather extensive detail. This is all very desirable because these items help determine what can and can not be accomplished with the racquet during contact.

Whether or not they are as good as can be is measured not by their conformance to style but by their contribution to the success of the hit as established during the period of contact. Workable concepts of the nature of that interval and of the hit must be developed before it is possible to optimize the processes and the timing that together make up a swing. It is thus necessary to know a little about the intricacies of that very miniscule slice of time, if not intuitively and automatically then via analytic examination.

MINISCULE BUT SIGNIFICANT

It might be said: "Who cares? It all occurs in a flash. You can't do anything about that thousandth or whatever part of a second anyway." But a hit involves more than just the act of instantaneously reversing the course of the ball. The interval of contact of racquet and ball covers a finite and extendable slice of time during which an all important sequence of actions and reactions take place. Though the period of contact is seemingly insignificant in duration the events within are nevertheless paramount in importance.

What occurs therein can explain the secrets for pace, accuracy, spin, feel, efficient use of energy, shock to the arm, etc. Even a person's intentions, expectations, and style are basically dependant on the understandings, misunderstandings, or just ignorance of the processes that operate during contact. So if the net results of a hit are good the explanations are to be found within that period, and if bad it had better be possible to make changes therein.

The pattern of a stroke in the case of an ineffective player and an expert may sometimes look quite similar. But the differences that are present during contact determine who is who. This should become very apparent as the elastic processes are discussed in the following paragraphs, and as the practical applications are developed in the succeeding chapters.

The ideas that will be presented can be used both as guidelines for execution and as standards for the purposes of correction. The understanding of the mechanics of a hit is also useful in insuring that any changes will be directed toward improvement, otherwise there are apt to be changes in the other direction.

INITIAL ASSUMPTIONS

In order to simplify the following discussion of elasticity it will be assumed that a "flat" shot (without spin) is used. Also assumed is that the preparation, path of the swing, hitting point, follow-through, attitude of the racquet during contact, and all other such details are considered to have been perfect unless specifically indicated otherwise. Elasticities themselves are considered to be perfect, and air resistance to be zero.

The purpose of these assumptions is to concentrate on the characteristics and essentials of the hit under ideal circumstances, and to postpone qualifications until later. Some of the statements are generalized, and though accurate enough for the present purpose they should not be considered as furnishing a technically complete picture of all the actions and reactions.

WHEN THE RACQUET MEETS A STATIONARY BALL

In the first example of a hit to be discussed the ball will be assumed to have zero initial velocity, as in a serve or as when the ball hits the ground in such a way as to bounce vertically to a convenient height. We will first consider the effects of the elasticity of the ball alone, as if those of the racquet and strings were not involved in the process.

When the racquet just begins to touch a stationary ball, say at 20 miles per hour (20 mph), the ball at first hardly moves because of having inertia, which here is resistance to change in motion from a state of rest. At this instant the cover on the side that is being hit begins to flatten, while the areas to the sides and front begin to bulge out. The flattening and bulging processes continue all the while that the ball gathers speed until it begins to be carried along at racquet velocity, 20 mph in this case. Now some strange processes begin to operate.

Due to the assumed perfect elasticity the stored energy is the equivalent of the full initial velocity of the racquet with respect to the ball, 20 mph here. This represents a potentially recoverable velocity apart from the existing ball velocity of the same amount, which latter is due to the ball being carried along at racquet speed. Since the ball was assumed to be initially stationary the stored energy was actually all derived from racquet velocity. But for technical reasons the stored energy is measured in terms of ball mass and velocity, not racquet.

With the racquet and ball moving forward together at 20 mph the cover begins to restore from being flattened on the one side and bulged out elsewhere to becoming round again. In snapping back into its original shape the back cover pushes off against the racquet, causing the rest of the ball to pick up speed and actually move faster than either the frame of the racquet or the back cover of the ball. This velocity generated by the rounding out of the ball is added to the existing going rate of 20 mph, which was derived simply from the ball being carried along at racquet speed.

If the cover were perfectly elastic all the energy taken up in the storage process would be converted into ball velocity without any loss as the ball regained its original round shape. Since in fact we assumed that ideal type of elasticity, as well as the benefits of a perfectly executed hit whatever that entails, we can say that all of the impact velocity (20 mph) gets to be recovered and is added to the carrying velocity (also 20 mph). Therefore after that recovery the ball would be moving forward at 40 mph even though the racquet continued along at the original rate of only 20 mph.

Looking at the same type of situation in another way: if you are riding in a van moving at 20 mph as it strikes a stationary ball you will see, if you have good enough eyesight, the ball first deform and then recover in shape as it bounces away from the van at a speed of 20 mph. But since you are observing the ball move away from the van at 20 mph while the van itself is moving in the same direction at 20 mph with respect to the ground, the total velocity of the ball with respect to the ground is the sum of the two, or 40 mph. But only in the never never land of perfect elasticity.

WHEN A MOVING BALL MEETS A STATIONARY RACQUET

In the above example we assumed initial velocities of zero for the ball and 20 miles per hour for the racquet. If the roles are reversed, with a ball having a speed of 20 mph meeting a racquet that is held stationary, the ball would still bounce off at the full 20 mph with respect to the racquet, the same as before. But since in this case the velocity at which the ball is being carried along by the racquet is zero, that amount, zero, added to the velocity developed from the energy stored in the elasticities, 20 nph, gives a sum that remains at 20 mph with respect to the ground rather than is increased to 40 mph as in the previous example, which involved a moving racquet.

WHEN A MOVING RACQUET MEETS A MOVING BALL

If the ball and racquet are approaching each other and are both moving at 20 mph with respect to the ground, the velocity relative to each other is the sum of the two ground speeds, giving an impact velocity of 40 mph and resulting in an equivalent amount of energy being stored in the elasticities.

When the flattening of the ball reaches its maximum the ball is again carried along at racquet speed, which was defined as 20 mph the same as in the first case. With the recovery of one hundred percent of the stored energy, 40 mph, the velocity of the ball as it leaves in the reverse direction is 40 mph with respect to the racquet but 60 mph with respect to the ground.

THE FORMULA FOR BALL VELOCITY

To simplify: final ball velocity with respect to the ground, in the realm of perfect elasticity only, equals ball velocity plus two times racquet velocity. The conversion of a moderate and easily developed speed in the racquet into premium grade pace for the ball is a very fortunate and phenomenal circumstance. But the extra velocity is not free since it is supplied by the player in moving the racquet.

In the real world the velocity will not be increased as efficiently as described, and the amount of enhancement will vary from about sixty percent of the total initial energy to practically nothing at all. The limiting factors will be explained in more detail in this and other chapters.

While according to the formula racquet velocity seems to have more importance than oncoming ball velocity, let it not be assumed that racquet motion must be maximized as much as possible, and that other requirements can be correspondingly compromised. As will be developed, the optimum use of the elastic processes involves conditions and results not at all in keeping with the seemingly simple implications of the formula.

PROGRESSIVE INCREASES IN PACE

An interesting application of the formula is as follows. Assume that ball and racquet both move at 20 mph with respect to the ground as they approach each other. This causes the ball to return at 60 mph, per the reasoning above. Then if the opponent's racquet is again moving at 20 mph when it meets the ball the resulting speed of the ball off the opponent's racquet would be 100 mph (ball velocity of 60 plus two times racquet velocity of 20). In the theoretical world of perfect elasticity this increment of 40 mph would continue to occur on each hit if each player just maintained a racquet speed of 20 mph.

Although the theory promises this really marvelous bonus from the elasticities there are other factors in the real world that put sudden and severe limits on attainability. The losses are due to friction, the physical limitations of the body, imperfections in the elasticity and the techniques, and the elastic limits of the materials in the racquet and the ball. The percentage of energy recovered in the case of a fast traveling ball would be less than for a slow, mainly because of greater frictional losses and because the ball would go out of contact earlier in the recovery process than for a slower moving ball.

The inefficiencies cause the progressive increases in speed to terminate so very soon that players simply do not become aware of the described phenomena. By not knowing about the theory they may fail to understand the implications and derive the advantages. But it can now begin to be understood how a relaxed and seemingly rather moderately paced swing can produce explosive ball speeds.

PRACTICAL UTILIZATION OF RACQUET VELOCITY

The more pace an approaching ball has the less velocity can be given to the racquet before exceeding the maximum impact velocity that a given player is capable of handling, and that the elasticities are capable of storing and reconverting efficiently. When a player swings the racquet just as hard as possible then any pace at all on the approaching ball, or just the inertia of a stationary ball, is by definition already in excess of the maximum impact velocity that the player can handle.

There is no reserve strength available to counteract either the inertia of a stationary ball or the momentum of a moving ball, as the case may be. As a consequence the racquet will be knocked backward very momentarily with respect to the arm, causing a great loss of pace and accuracy and probably placing heavy strain on both the wrist and arm as well. One side lesson that can be learned therefrom is that it is a great mistake to let annoyance at the tactics of an opponent, or an excessive urge to win the point, trigger an attempt to blast the ball back with the use of all the strength that a person is capable of mustering.

Players with the right instincts adjust the swing so that the racquet velocity with respect to the ball does not create an impact that is greater than can be successfully countered with reserve strength. Less talented players may either just freeze the arm defensively or jerk the racquet around in an ever more convulsive, unprofitable, and unreasonable manner in spite of thousands of previous unhappy experiences. By not knowing of the inefficiencies they may fail to realize that adding more than enough to racquet velocity only means that a great deal of the energy will just get to be dissipated and lost.

The arm can swing the racquet at high speeds but cannot at the same time also resist the impact of the ball and fulfill other conditions still to be discussed. So it is not necessary or desirable to maximize racquet velocity if the approaching ball has any appreciable pace. The lesson as to handling fast balls is not "hit like hell." You don't have to hit harder and harder the faster and faster the ball comes. Just the opposite.

The gains predicted by the formula also signify that there is that much to be lost in unrealized enhancement in the speed of the ball above the carrying velocity of the racquet if there is inadequate accommodation to all of the characteristics of elasticity. Therein can be found both the explanations for disappointing results and the means for advancement to higher levels. In the real world the potential gain would not be as much as given by the formula and therefore neither would the potential loss.

THE PROBLEM OF MAXIMIZING THE RECOVERY OF ENERGY

The above phrase "inadequate accommodation" is meant to imply that other factors besides racquet speed are involved in recovering energy from the elasticities. Not satisfying these other conditions will result in the failure to obtain more than an insignificant part of the benefits specified by the formula. Even the selection of a perfectly appropriate average racquet velocity for a particular shot is still far from enough to insure a proper hit.

In the previously discussed imaginary world of perfect elasticity the cover of the ball would have to be weightless, and would have to be able to change from being flat on one side to becoming perfectly round

17

again without overshooting that state. In the real world the cover has weight, in fact almost all the weight of the ball. Consequently, when the flattened cover rebounds to its original round shape it doesn't stop there but is carried a little further because, like any moving mass, it has momentum.

The momentum causes the cover to overshoot its normal position, reverse, overshoot again and continue in diminishing oscillations until the stored energy is used up, mostly in internal friction. Unless the player uses appropriate techniques to dampen at least some of the initial overshoot there will be a big waste of energy, and with it goes the enhancement of pace predicted by the formula. The partial solution, and that is all that can be hoped for, is to keep the racquet pressed against the ball. But that is quite difficult to do.

EFFECTS OF ACCELERATING THE RACQUET

The solution to maximizing the recovery of energy is to try to accelerate the racquet progressively in an effort to extend contact by compensating for the ball picking up speed relative to the racquet. There should not be a constant racquet velocity, or a hurrying of the racquet either, but rather a smooth, controlled, continuous, and almost imperceptible acceleration. One of the biggest mistakes, as always, is to overdo things.

Maintaining acceleration through contact implies moving the racquet at less than maximum during any part of the stroke, and especially during the early stages. It is wrong to confront the ball with maximum racquet velocity at the initial instant of impact. A hit involves not a slap at the ball nor a maximum velocity swing into impact, but a hardly perceptible development of racquet momentum in the direction of the hit throughout the swing, including the interval of contact. To be effective during contact the acceleration has to carry slightly into the follow-through.

It is thus necessary to recover energies at higher racquet velocities than that at which the energies were stored. Energy is being stored if the racquet is moving faster than the ball, otherwise energy is being recovered as long as contact is maintained. After that any remaining stored energy is lost. Contact will be broken too soon if the racquet velocity is constant or is slowing down.

A MINISCULE INTERVAL

At this point there ought to be a well justified doubt about the validity of the above reasoning in the light of the minute amount of acceleration possible in a very miniscule interval of time. The defense is that if any acceleration at all is obtained a proportionate amount of it occurs in every slice of time, no matter how small. Contact will be extended thereby albeit minutely, and every little bit is important because both the storage and the recovery of energy via the elasticities also extend over very minute slices of time.

It is obvious that the cover of the ball goes through the two distinct stages of flattening and recovery during the seemingly insignificant contact interval. The amount of stored energy that gets converted into ball velocity is based on the success in keeping the racquet in contact so as to maximize the length of that interval. The factors that lengthen the interval add to the storage period as well as to the recovery period. As can be seen, the method of developing racquet momentum is as important as how much is developed.

The behavior of the elasticities is not limited by the amount of time available during contact because the operation of the elasticities determines the length of that interval. If the elasticities required more time than is available in the perceived interval of contact to both store energy and reconvert a good part of it into ball velocity then that interval would simply be longer.

CONCLUSIONS

When the racquet velocity is maximized to the extent that there is not enough reserve strength left to both maintain a gradual acceleration and counter the impact of the ball much of the potential velocity is wasted. The storage process is then inefficient and the recovery process incomplete. To get the greatest ball velocity with the least effort it is necessary to distribute the available effort over both the storage and recovery operations.

Maximizing the initial impact, as is the common tendency, allots all of the energy to only the first part of the job, storage. That mitigates not only against adequate recovery but other elements as well, such as maintaining accuracy and control, reinforcing the arm with the body, minimizing shock and effort, etc. So just a warning at this time: it is a mistake to overemphasize anything since no one element deserves all the attention and effort.

The only available means to optimize a hit is to utilize the properties of elasticity in the most advantageous way. It follows that learning to hit properly and getting rid of bad habits can usually proceed on a sounder basis through a knowledge of the characteristics of elasticity than through the repetition of patterns, aimless variation, uninformed observation, etc. By the time other discussions are finished it should begin to be understood why vicious slaps and other common habits produce weak shots and high rates of error.

When a game needs improvement, at any level of play, a common procedure is to analyze the actions for violations of accepted patterns. Since this is not the same as examining a stroke with respect to the principles of hitting it cannot be expected that even with apparent improvement in form there may not nevertheless be an adverse effect on the results. If nothing else, the strokes could become more artificial, and the processes for the storage and recovery of energy could be harmfully affected in subtle ways. It must be remembered that even the games of many of the most successful pros differ markedly from the norms, and that the pros have their own ways of extracting as much as they can from the elasticities, some with more success than others.

It ought now to be apparent that technical knowledge can help a tennis game, and that a player, especially one having difficulties, should be very concerned about the techniques for maximizing the contact interval. Even patterns themselves can be refined and made more effective by being based on the principles of elasticity rather than on abstract classic traditions, regardless of how close the two results might eventually come to coincide.

The dismal results of improper execution need not be dismissed as lack of talent, but can begin to be related to the specific swing used and the violations of the laws of elasticity that are bound to occur to some extent. As the understandings are improved there will be increased success in interpreting good and bad results, and in developing new understandings.

Corrective measures intended for more effective recovery of energy, more accuracy, fun, etc., will not only work but will stand a good chance of gaining ready acceptance in the player's way of thinking. Not insignificantly, false remedies and illusions will no longer find similar acceptance. The mind is involved in the execution of a stroke. Therefor the player must be convinced of the validity of the reasons for doing things in new ways.

Analysis, description, demonstration, emulation, etc., provide the ostensibly sufficient tools for instruction. But it is the understanding of the physical processes that occur during contact that is the essential element in the ability to evaluate results, relate consequences to causes, determine what is missing, what needs correction, what will work and what will not. The rules and recommendations given so far should not be taken as restrictions under all conditions. There has to be a freedom to use for the needs of the moment what under ideal circumstances would be considered undesirable.

chapter three

other elasticities

Thus far the only elasticity that has been discussed has been that of the ball. It is admittedly very important as anyone discovers when hitting a ball that has lost some of its pressure, or even when using a brand that is either bouncier or the reverse of the one a person happens to be accustomed to. The elasticity of the ball stores an important part of the energy of a hit, but there are other elasticities that store appreciable amounts of energy and ought to be looked into as well. They are the elasticities of the strings and of the frame of the racquet.

FAST RECOVERY OF THE STRINGS

While the strings do not absorb and store as much energy as the ball they have special importance because of having very little weight and internal friction, and also a very fast recovery, much more so than the ball. So the strings are both the first to return to their original shape and the best at giving back a major percentage of the energy that they absorb. They act to increase the speed of the ball above the carrying velocity of the racquet in a manner similar to but independent of the rounding out of the ball.

The early recovery of the strings causes an enhancement of the pace of the ball that tends to send the ball out of contact before the energies stored in the elasticities of the ball and the racquet have also been reconverted into ball velocity. Since the latter two devices store more than half of the total energy involved, the quick departure of the ball due to the fast response of the strings places special importance on trying to maintain and extend contact by accelerating the racquet through that interval. Precaution must be taken that the action is slight, smooth, and continuous, not sudden and impulsive.

The partially sequential type of recovery involved with the different elasticities does not change the nature of the recovery process, and does not change the formula that has been previously described for the enhancement of the pace of the ball. That formula refers to the cumulative overall effect and not separately to each individual elasticity. The maximum theoretical departing ball velocity is still oncoming ball velocity plus two times racquet velocity. But the actual efficiency of the equipment limits the recovery of energy to at best about sixty percent of what is theoretically available, and to much less than that if the ball is hit very hard.

STRING TENSION

The tighter or shorter the strings the faster do they recover, but the less energy gets stored in them, the less is available for conversion into ball velocity, and the sooner is the limit of the string's elasticity reached. The effect of that limit in this case is not inelastic stretching but mostly just a restriction on the amount of energy that the strings are able to absorb.

Conversely, the looser or longer the strings the greater is the percentage of the total amount of energy that can be stored in them and the longer will it take for the strings to recover (although still extremely quickly). There is another advantage in the longer recovery time for the strings in that the recovery is more nearly simultaneous with that of the ball. However the strings are not elastic at all degrees of looseness. They have to be tight enough to be slightly stretched. Otherwise there is a great loss of energy at impact in merely bringing the strings to a slightly stretched condition.

The fact that short or very tight strings store less energy than long or moderately tensioned strings does not mean that the energy not taken up in the strings is lost. Most of the remainder is merely absorbed by the other less efficient elasticities: bending of the racquet and flattening of the ball. There is more energy loss in these two due to the presence of more weight and internal friction than there is in the strings. Thus they convert a lower percentage of the stored energy into ball velocity than do the strings, but not to a degree that constitutes a serious problem.

Two other very noticeable effects that go with various string tensions are changes in the feel and in the degree of control. These may or may not suit the player's preferences or style of play. Contrary to popular belief, control does not seem to increase with tightness. This is because very tight strings reflect errors fairly accurately, somewhat as a mirror reflects light, whereas moderately tensioned strings tend to be more "forgiving." The chapter on "RACQUET ATTITUDE" contains an analysis of the rebound angle.

An undesirable consequence of looseness is a corresponding increase in the amount of slippage between the horizontal and vertical strings. Slippage is the major factor of wear since the strings tend to cut through each other as they slide back and forth at each hit. For that reason recreational players often choose a tension that is tight enough so that the slippage does not become excessive even after a normal slight loss of tension as a result of play.

Plastic inserts are available for placement at the cross points to minimize slippage. There is some loss in response due to the frictional losses that occur as the strings slide through the grooves of the devices. Strings slide over each over with much less friction and loss of energy than they do through the grooves of the inserts. The effect on the response of the strings is not appreciable unless the inserts are used in large numbers. They can be cemented in place to eliminate this type of frictional loss.

RACQUET ELASTICITY

The racquet frame stores energy by becoming bent, and the recovery of energy occurs as the frame snaps forward out of its bent back condition. The velocity of the forward rebound of the racquet head is again additional to the overall forward movement of the frame, and thus adds to the velocity of the ball in the same manner as discussed for the rounding of the ball and the snapping back of the strings.

Although racquets of different sizes or materials may have the same elasticity they will differ in internal friction, affecting the efficiency, quickness of response, and damping characteristics. The preferences as to the material, stiffness, and design of the racquet depend mostly on a person's game, likes, and dislikes. For instance, a person with a quick swing may like to use a stiff racquet (with quick recovery), but then again may find the shock to the arm to be more unpleasant than with a flexible frame.

Large racquets and long strings store more energy but have more air resistance than do the lesser. And large frames have a large rotational inertia. This is also true of racquets with extra weights at the edges of the frame. Rotational inertia is useful in countering torque on off center hits, but requires expenditure of extra strength and energy for any manipulation of the attitude of the racquet.

THE RECOVERY SEQUENCE

Since all the elasticities behave the same in terms of enhancing ball velocity above the overall velocity of the racquet it doesn't really matter which recovers first. One major preference is to recover energy first from the elasticity having the least loss. This does happen since the strings recover first and are also the most efficient.

Another preference is to recover as completely as possible from the elasticity that stores the most energy, which is the ball. But there is no way to control the sequence of the processes other than to use the type of ball, racquet, strings, tension of strings, and manner of hitting that seem to give the best results.

PRACTICAL CONSEQUENCES

The above information is further evidence that a knowledge of the behavior of elasticities can help a player develop techniques that optimize results. Other benefits include helping to identify, interpret, and correct flaws, and to understand the requirements for timing, acceleration of the racquet, follow-through, etc. The knowledge can also help in interpreting the feel of the strokes, a very useful indicator as will become apparent in succeeding chapters.

Many people assume, not unreasonably, that in an interval as small as that of contact it is not possible to have a sequence of discrete events such as the succession of recoveries for the different types of elasticities. Yet they are there, and not only in tennis but in all other hitting sports as well. In golf and baseball the elasticities of the equipment are so slight that the storage and recovery of energy occur in a fraction of the time that it takes in tennis.

In baseball the wood fibers of the bat deflect very minutely and quickly, but nevertheless function exactly like the strings of a racquet in the storage and recovery processes. The bending of the bat is of course exactly synonymous with the bending of the racquet. Note when bat meets ball the much greater velocity of the ball than that of the bat, and how the ball is well on its way before the bat has gone more than a little past contact in the forward swing.

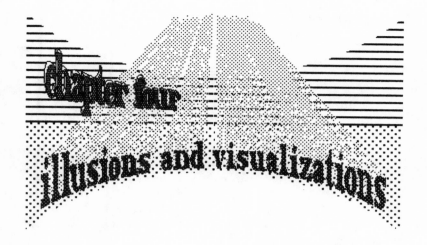

chapter four

illusions and visualizations

Many mediocre players have heard or read of most if not all of even the fine points that coaches discuss when giving lessons. But applying that information to bring about improvements in established games is an entirely different matter. Even a thorough knowledge of the characteristics of expert level strokes is not enough to insure that a person will thereby become or remain an accomplished tennis player. Therefore before going on in the following chapters to consider how a knowledge of the characteristics of elasticity can be used to optimize hitting techniques it is well to study the impact of several other influences, and how they can either hinder or promote improvement.

In the first chapter the anomaly was mentioned that bad tennis habits creep in very easily while desired corrections are made with great difficulty if at all. This would suggest that there is a special importance to understanding the means by which bad habits are perpetuated and generated. There is a constant battle to minimize reversion to old bad habits and intrusion of some that are new even after high level strokes have been mastered.

UNREAL GOALS

A common source of many player's problems is the presence of mental concepts of hits beyond athletic capabilities and physical realities, what is defined here for the purposes of this book as "illusions." One typical illusion would have the ball disappear across the court as fast as thought. This might seem to evidence a disordered mind, but such desires not only control just about every shot of some otherwise very rational and intelligent recreational players but an occasional shot by the experts as well.

For people whose play is controlled at least in part by such notions, which includes most of us, results judged to be first rate by rational standards do not come close to measuring up to the much more compelling ideas conjured up by mental fancies. Understandably, the practical reality is treated as an unacceptable substitute, not consciously but through the controlling influence of the inner values.

Unless the illusions can be thoroughly understood and discredited the unrealistic expectations will continue to trigger the habitual impractical responses. This does not mean that coaches must then act as psychologists, but that players must be made fully aware of some of the detrimental consequences of certain mental attitudes. The main antidotes for the unwarranted faith people place in their follies include an awareness of the role of urges and emotions in connection with their personal set of valid techniques and wild idiosyncrasies.

Beyond that it is necessary to know which characteristics of stroke production are really synonymous with the best results, and to have a reasonably accurate intuitive or factual understanding of the elastic processes.

Only then will there be a good chance that the reality can come to be appreciated more than the mere fantasy.

INABILITY TO FACE THE FACTS

There seems to be more numerous wrong ways to do things in recreational level tennis than in any other sport. Some of the methods are so spectacular that there would be a great incentive for change if the player could merely accurately picture what the self and the swing looked like on each shot, and could then also assess and admit the extent by which the real results failed to meet the wild expectations. Unfortunately the reality of what actually happens is often far different from what the player believes happens.

The same can be said for what is physically possible and what many players mistakenly believe to be possible, or play as if they seem to believe it were so. In light of some of the varieties of inappropriate techniques one sees, and to an alarming extent uses, it is apparent that what is commonly expected of a stroke often amounts to illusions.

That remark is not intended to be derogatory of recreational tennis but merely a necessary recognition of the fact that substantial numbers of people are blind to the complete irrationality of some of their techniques. They apparently lack, or pay no attention to, the natural feedback mechanisms by which the feelings of good or bad hits should exert their appropriate influence on subsequent execution. Even the most inept players entertain some hope of acquiring the better shots some fine day. But giving up their unrealistic objectives is not part of the bargain, however poor the current results and unpleasant the feel.

MENTAL PICTURES

Most players who have not seen themselves on video have serious misconceptions about how they actually play. They are apt to overestimate their degree of conformance to good style and to be only vaguely aware, if at all, of conspicuous deviations. And even seeing a replay on video does not necessarily equate to realistic evaluation, or result in a serious attempt to switch to preferable alternatives.

At the other end of the scale, if you do not have a pretty good idea of how an exceptionally fine shot was just made you are at as much a loss to know how you can make that fortunate event happen again. If you don't have an accurate idea of what your strokes and your flaws look like, or don't get feedback through monitoring the feel of the hit, or don't know what constitutes a good hit, it follows that you are in a poor position to make corrections to your game. The awareness of the feel is a most important factor in evaluating a previous shot, controlling the intents for a coming shot, or developing the images for an improved technique.

In order to recognize and correct the flaws that have just occurred, or to reflect on something good that ought to be remembered for future use, it is desirable to be able to visualize and reenact the complete action involved in the last stroke as if having watched it as an observer or experienced it as the player. This calls for reconstruction of what the shot looked like from remembrances of what it felt like. The term to be used here to cover the reconstruction in the mind of an action that has occurred, good or bad, or to picture a coming action as it should occur or is intended to occur, will be "visualization."

This invoking of an image of the past or of the future can be very useful, but it is not as easy to accomplish as one may think. It is in a way only a substitute for the use of video recordings. But it has the special advantages that it can be used at any time, can be more complete because it is internal, can be projected for a coming stroke instead of being limited to recalling the past, and can provide some mental equivalents of experiencing the feel.

One way to practice visualization is to once in a while try to mimic the entire sequence of a stroke just exactly as it happened, not sparing a single trivial or unpleasant detail, but not exaggerating them either. On each reenactment or visualization consider in the background of the mind whether it would be desirable to reexperience that shot done the same way. A disregard of the feel and of the consequences, and control instead by subconscious intent, is exactly what happens over and over without awareness or analysis.

Visualizing a replay of those situations in which a shot was flubbed can be especially useful. It can be very revealing as to the errors of both commission and omission. In some cases the most valuable outcome of the mental reexperience of a past shot is a downward reevaluation of the satisfactions derived from an apparently effective hit that did not also have a satisfying feel, or that compared poorly with the ideal.

If you can correctly visualize how the stroke should look you have succeeded to some extent in installing the mental controls to hit that way. A piecemeal approach to the elimination of flaws and to the building of a more desirable style may not then be necessary. In applying this method the procedure amounts to something like getting the body ready to act out the stroke as visualized, sort of like trying to imitate a mental picture in every respect.

This preparatory visualization puts the intentions under the control of more ambitious yet more rational expectations than the ones automatically conjured up by habits, urges, fears, and illusions. Taking at least a little control away from those all powerful influences is a primary and essential prerequisite to change. Tennis should be more a matter of living up to ideals than being controlled by unsound ideas, unnecessary doubts, and irrational expectations.

Refinements can be gradually developed in the idea of a proper stroke through the preliminary visualizations combined with feedback from the actual hits. Improvements in the visualized stroke are very necessary since the stroke cannot be better than the idea of it. The technique of progressive refinement of the concepts has the additional advantage that it continues to operate in raising the level of a game even as the player advances to successively higher levels of competence. Unfortunately for self-satisfaction, but fortunately for continued progress, there is also a simultaneous heightened awareness of one's remaining shortcomings.

MENTAL PRACTICE

A further extension of the process of visualization is to practice a sequence of strokes mentally: imagining the involvement of the body in the swing, moving into position, getting body and racquet ready, swinging freely but not wildly, making adjustments, repeating the stroke to iron out difficulties, etc. A return can be imagined from the opponent in a way that is very difficult to handle. Then the intentions for the swing to be used can be imagined, getting ready according to those intentions, and so on.

Most players will probably be surprised at how one's real faults creep in, and how difficult the mental gymnastics involved with the attempt to eliminate the counterparts of the physical faults from the mental pictures. Visualizing oneself as an observer watching someone else make the shot in exactly the same way can lessen this effect.

The fact that the pictures tend to have the same characteristics and persistence as the real habits is more helpful than not. It makes it possible to work on the whole stroke mentally. A new type of visualization can be introduced to make that task easier: visualization of the action in "slow motion," abbreviated "SMV."

This can be of help for several reasons: (1) the slow pace of the swing is the antithesis of muscling the shot, (2) the smooth relaxed flow corresponds to that found in really fine strokes, and (3) many compensations and idiosyncrasies are somehow easily excluded, which is exactly what one wants to do but finds next to impossible to accomplish otherwise, either mentally or actually.

Initially the slow motion visualizations (SMV) will take some time. Ultimately they may occasionally take almost no time at all, sort of like the experience of some people of having their whole lives flash before their eyes in an instant. So before a stroke is actually executed it is possible to visualize it without the impulsive eccentricities that invariably seem to accompany full speed visualization or execution. If such corrections can be made to the mental image then the barriers to improvement to the real swing may also be removed.

It is very useful to make such attempts to train the automatic controls, whatever they are and wherever centered, instead of just futilely trying to drill habits into unknowing and unwilling muscles. The above described activities not only provide such training but tend to replace the previously discussed "illusions" with "visualizations." In a sense a stroke is merely the set of images and intentions that dictate a set of mechanical responses. Important to the mentioned mental factors are those that are missing, as well as those that are not but ought to be.

ANTICIPATION AND PREPARATION

One of the prominent differences between what did and what should happen will very often be in the preparation for the shot. The plain fact is that the inadequate extent to which the mind, feet, body, arm, and racquet are made ready often precludes a genuinely good stroke before the forward swing has even started.

Much lack of talent is merely inadequate preparation. A good preparation should in itself be one of the satisfying experiences that a person expects to get out of a stroke. The first and most important phase is mental, but most players are too busy agonizing over the results of past events, or entertaining illusions about the results desired from the next, to do any anticipating of the manner of getting ready to accomplish a satisfactory hit.

Examples of the consequences of inadequate preparation are the use of improvisations in the grip, swing, hitting point, etc., to compensate for a happenstance initial position and a compromised readiness for the shot. A more subtle consequence can be an ostensibly normal looking hit but one without appreciable power.

The arm and body must get fully ready for the forward swing, not just half ready. If you don't realize that you were not quite properly ready, not just ostensibly in terms of just having the racquet back but also in terms of intending to do things according to your best present understandings of a hit, you may waste a lot of time looking for remedies for other flaws, or resort to strange and convulsive attempts to develop respectable results, merely because of a relatively simple initial problem with readiness.

Notes on

chapter five

compensations

Ideally each element of a stroke should have value in one of three ways: by directly fulfilling or helping to fulfill a function, by being a part of the preparation for a desirable manner of execution of a directly useful element, or by being a part of the natural ending of the same. Any particular action if not actually justifiable in any of the above ways should at least be neutral in the sense of not detracting from or interfering with elements that are useful.

In reality no stroke can be executed that well, but even with an allowance for a large degree of imperfection it is still hard to explain the strange antics and flourishes that dominate the strokes of many players. In order to find the means to deal with these personal eccentricities it is necessary to try to analyze the rationale behind their origin and use.

INSTINCTIVE CORRECTIONS

Unexpectedly enough though, there can be useful aspects to some apparently purposeless manipulations of the racquet. When any directly functional element of a stroke is omitted or is not executed properly the natural result would be a miss-hit unless something not normal to the stroke is inserted as a remedy. The term "compensations" will be used here for these automatic adjustments or manipulations introduced to avoid the harmful results of real or perceived deficiencies in techniques or capabilities.

Such makeshift remedies are just by the nature of their origin created not consciously and wisely but automatically and unwittingly, and thus will often be something that is a far cry from what the coach would recommend, or even what the player would voluntarily select. An unfortunate corollary is that such adjustments are in effect merely crutches used to make it possible to live with the underlying problems instead of having to get rid of them.

THE WORKINGS OF COMPENSATIONS

It is obvious, for example, that if a player is in a wrong position but swings as if from a proper position the ball will have to go wrong. If the mentioned basic problem is not recognized and remedied then some of the correctness must be taken out of the swing, and sufficient other related compensations devised which, though perhaps bizarre in themselves, nevertheless make it possible to get by with being in an improper position.

But if a hit is made under conditions that are not compatible with a proper swing then the player is merely developing and reinforcing a compromised technique. It is by this type of circumstance that involuntary and unwelcome idiosyncrasies become permanent and prominent characteristics of many player's games. There are problems enough in getting the most out of a particular style of play without saddling it with compromises whose sole purpose is to permit the retention of harmful or at least unproductive peculiarities.

As a corollary, seemingly extraneous manipulations may in reality be easy-way-out compensations for flaws that the player may not even be aware of. Therefor the recognition of an extraneous manipulation as being a compensation could be of use in identifying the underlying fault. At any rate compensations cannot usually just be ignored. There almost always are harmful effects on the stroke, as well as the potentially even more serious consequences of generating other compensations and allowing perpetuation of the underlying problems.

SUPPRESSING COMPENSATIONS

It is generally not a sufficient remedy merely to tell the student to get rid of a seemingly meaningless manipulation of the racquet, or elbow, or feet, etc. If, as is often the case, the action is in fact of the nature of a compensation then the more rational approach would be to try to make the compensations and adaptations unnecessary by eliminating the responsible basic flaws. Otherwise the player will be compelled to retain the compensations, not because of stupidity or stubbornness but out of necessity.

If the basic flaw cannot be identified it may be possible to force the issue by consciously refusing to continue the use of the unaccountable idiosyncrasy. In other words, suspend the use of the compensation and let the ball go wrong if it will, and then search back to try to find the one or more basic problems in the execution that caused the ball to go astray, and for which result the now suppressed compensation had provided corrections. This may not be easy because flaws usually exist in layers.

An additional task is to also determine whether the ostensible flaw is a desirable feature that ought to be retained or a defect that ought to be eliminated. One of the most notable examples of this type of dilemma pertained to the use of the Western forehand grip, which at one time was thought to be an anomaly that anybody taking lessons at any level should be compelled to discontinue. And now the grip is one of the popular standards.

THE ORIGINS OF COMPENSATIONS

The usual reasons why players find themselves compelled to make surreptitious adjustments to their stroke patterns, besides an inner awareness of incompatibilities between elements, are the desire for an incredible result or the feeling of a need to disguise a personal athletic deficiency. The adjustments are automatic and not preplanned, and are therefore little affected by attempts to impose conscious mental controls.

An example of a compensation induced by an incompatibility is when on the serve a player turns the body around to face the net too much or too soon, and has to shift the grip around in mid-swing from the standard grip to one that is more suitable for use with the suddenly open stance. The compensation might not be known to the player or be apparent to an observer. But if some adjustment is not made, such as shifting the grip or turning the wrist, the racquet will be faced in the wrong direction. So an accommodation is developed for a problem with the racquet attitude arising out of a more basic defect. This converts one defect into two.

When corrective manipulations are introduced on a one time basis in reaction to emergency circumstances those actions are expedients rather than compensations. Both the compensations and the expedients can be considered to have a useful function, even though merely of the nature of attempting to diminish the penalties for violations of the rules of elasticity and stroke production.

Occasionally a perceived problem will be just a misconception as to the technique required to produce a certain result. Or it may be an imagined defect, as when some people feel that they are not physically strong enough to hit with good pace, and must resort to enhanced efforts and special manipulations to obtain a ball velocity that in reality should not be a problem even for people with frail physiques. Henry Ford is quoted as having said "Whether you think you can or think you can't, you're right." The "I can't" attitude, justified or not, automatically causes the introduction of compensations as if for a real deficiency. However, the majority of problems are real enough, although perhaps not exactly easy to identify.

As long as the fundamental execution is faulty there will be a need to retain the corresponding collection of compensations. The same will be true if there is a desire for some unattainable effect, or to procure some nonexistent benefit from a violent technique, or to conceal a real or fancied flaw or athletic inadequacy.

A SENSE OF DEPRIVATION

Players develop a sense of dependence on habits, even those that are bad. So to remove one basic flaw and just one consequent compensation requires not only the suppression of those two largely automatic actions but then having to put up with a feeling of deprivation of each of them.

So even in the case of a simple flaw and one associated compensation, and with no interactions with other elements of the stroke, there are four forces prejudicing the player against any change: the flaw, the compensation, and the feeling of deprivation of each. Notice, for instance, how hard it seems to be for players to get rid of the useless habit that some have of dipping slightly at the knees just before the toss for the serve.

The complications are further compounded by the fact that the faults, compensations, and deprivations interact with each other. Add to this the fact that the desired new habits and responses also present a challenge in themselves, and it becomes obvious that when players allow a faulty technique to become habit they have thereby created almost insurmountable obstacles to advancement to the next level of play. By the above reasoning, if a person has only a half dozen faults, and has just one compensation to go with each of them, the total number of forces opposing the introduction of just one correction for each of the six basic faults would amount to thirty.

When a new technique creates feelings of deprivation there will be a strong urge to get rid of them by retreating to the comfort of the bad habits. Unfortunately it is not likely that many players will become aware on their own that the cure does not come about through merely refusing to kowtow to the demands of habit and the feelings of deprivation. Players must progress in a positive sense by developing and recognizing satisfactions in the manner of execution and the feel of a really good hit.

CIRCUMVENTIONS

Problems and bad habits never seem to fade away, but just come back in new disguise. So although urges, flaws, or compensations may at times appear to be conquered they often return in modified form, and the players are right back where they started, out in the cold again. While reversion to the exact previous techniques may not actually take place it might just as well occur because the corresponding old results, errors, and inadequacies are there as if they had never been gone.

What happens is that the player may succeed in using an improved technique but is nevertheless very uncomfortable in living with it, largely because of the many feelings of deprivation, as discussed above. It therefore seems necessary to revert to the old ways without being very open about it. In other words, the new methods are ostensibly retained but means are found to circumvent them and bring back the old habits in disguised form. This helps explain why initial progress is often quickly followed by a sudden letdown.

An example of a circumvention is when a person with an inappropriate grip successfully switches to a new, but then becomes uncomfortable with the feel because the attitude of the racquet has been changed too. In this case the change of grip may be quite proper, but it is not compatible with the old flaws and compensations. A means will then ordinarily be invented to sort of regress, not to the former grip but the former attitude. This could possibly be done by a simple turn of the wrist. And then the old problems are likely to reappear even though the grip remains correct. A byproduct of such difficulties is a loss of confidence in the suitability of legitimate techniques.

A CARD HOUSE OF COMPENSATIONS

Consider a more complicated possible set of compensations. Conjecture that the real initial flaw consists of an eagerness to demolish the ball, and that it results in an extra quick swing. The fast swing in turn causes an early hit, which puts the contact point too far out in front. The arm has little remaining forward extension in that area and must begin to travel prematurely in the roundhouse or sideways direction.

When the hit is too far out in front on the classic type forehand the body interferes with the free movement of the arm in the latter stages of the swing. So the player may then unconsciously pull the front foot away from the path of the ball to eliminate interference by the body. But this rotates the body away from the hit and further opens the stance, aggravating the roundhouse and its effects.

If the grip used is for a swing from a sideways stance the attitude of the racquet would now be wrong. A new compensation would be required for this factor, and it could take the form of rotating the wrist upward to give the racquet a proper attitude. The wrist may also have to be bent backward to face the racquet in the desired forward direction rather than off toward the side. At the end of the swing the wrist might then be returned to normal by being rolled forward quickly, accompanied possibly with a simultaneous lifting of the elbow.

The most visible faults in this case would probably be the sideward movements of the racquet and the front foot, and the lift of the elbow. However the basic physical causes would be the quick swing and early hit, and these in turn would have a psychological origin in the form of an emotional urge to demolish the ball.

While the above sequence is only conjectural it is entirely realistic in respect to how problems and compensations get built up, and in how they can cause a game to fall apart. It is easy to see that a person who develops just a very few basic faults can soon end up with a game consisting mostly of compensations.

Granted that the use of a patterned swing would temporarily eliminate the physical flaws all at once, but it would not address the mentioned causes and the feelings of deprivation, so reversion would be practically guaranteed. A coach looking at the described stroke would probably not be able to deduce the relationships as just conjectured, and of course they would differ considerably from individual to individual. But it can be seen that piecemeal attention to the visible faults would not do much good.

NON-STANDARD NEED NOT BE NOT GOOD

Sometimes a seeming flaw is actually a refinement. An example is the habit of some top level players of stopping the swing on the serve a little more than half way down in front of the body, in other words cutting down on the follow-through. This constraint can also be seen on occasion on other strokes.

It may also be noticed that during the actual hit the expert will probably be bearing down as if fully intending a long follow-through. The usual main purpose of the partial deviation from good technique is to get ready as soon as possible for the return. By stopping the swing a little short something is lost in power, but for high level players it may be advisable to sacrifice some speed in order to ensure readiness for a possible sizzling reply from the opponent.

The swings cannot all be perfect, and each imperfect element may require corresponding accommodations in other associated elements. However, the same instincts that introduce compensations for wrong body position, swing of arm, etc., will also work to introduce accommodations corresponding to corrected body position, swing of arm, etc. However this is likely to happen only if the corrections are based on the combination of educated concepts, attitudes, intentions, and satisfactions. It is not enough to rely on the traditional approaches such as repetitive drill, emulation of patterns, or piecemeal correction of visible individual mannerisms.

Some flourishes are just that and nothing more, neither adding to nor subtracting from the effectiveness of the stroke, but merely satisfying a habit, image, or emotion. If the aesthetic effect is not too bad, and if no great amount of energy is wasted or strains created, then such flourishes can be allowed to remain so that more attention can be given to higher priority problems.

CORRECTIONS AFTER CONTACT

A different type of attempted correction has neither effectiveness nor a real function since it occurs after contact has ended, when the ball is no longer under the control of the racquet and may in fact be well on its way toward its destination. This type of behavior can be called "post-contact coercion." It is not necessarily harmless.

Examples of such actions in another sport, bowling, are the agonized contortions that many bowlers go through as the ball rolls steadily on, completely unaffected by the telepathic attempts to influence its path and destination. This particular type of physical agonizing is usually called "body English." In the case of the bowler, other than providing a little extra exercise, the body English has no beneficial or harmful effect. Basically similar maneuvers are sometimes seen in tennis on both serves and ground strokes, but are usually less visible because of the fast pace of the action.

HARMFUL EFFECTS OF COERCION

A post-contact coercion that seems harmless in itself may nevertheless not be tolerable, if only because it is unwise to be telegraphing remonstrances toward the last shot when there is a need to be getting ready for the next. More importantly, the coercive motion will probably not be entirely harmless if it was started or perhaps merely prepared for before contact was broken. An additional possibility is that a coercion may be used as a substitute for a needed real remedy. A post-contact coercion can therefore be much worse than just a useless gesture.

In citing specific examples of such attempted coercions only the type that might affect contact need be brought up. One common instance is holding back on the swing, as if to influence the ball similarly and keep it from sailing out. If nothing else this action will result in the slowing down of the racquet before and during contact. Spin and pace are reduced, and even if the ball lands in court the bounce is likely to be rather nice for the opponent to hit off of.

Another example is the turning of the racquet face over or under at the end of a swing, usually with the intention of instructing the ball how to behave in the vicinity of the net. However this type of manipulation is not always post-contact coercion. It could also be the natural ending of a compensation initiated during contact, or a part of some special technique needed for a specific purpose.

An action that may occur after contact, although it often occurs during, is a downward pull on the racquet at the end of the serve to persuade the ball to drop similarly downward as it passes the net. The results of stopping the racquet short or pulling it down are almost always counter to the intent. Besides reducing pace they tend to preclude the topspin that does help to bring the ball down in court.

THE PERCEIVED NEED

While there are some post-contact gestures that are no more than personal idiosyncrasies, most of them arise out of a desire to make after-the-deed corrections for something perceived to be undesirable in either the execution or the impending unpalatable and unavoidable result. Consequently the real cure for post-contact manipulations is to try to eliminate the cause of the perceived need.

But the correction of intents and minor flaws in execution is difficult because, for one thing, the problems are usually less visible than the compensations or coercions that they generate. Awareness of the details of one's own strokes requires a more thorough knowledge of the fundamental principles of hitting, and of the automatic generation of accommodations to poor techniques, than most players are likely to have.

REVISE THE SATISFACTIONS

Once a coercion is discovered, and if it seems to have harmful consequences, then the task is to identify and eliminate the cause rather than the resultant problem. Ordinarily the corrections will not take hold if introduced via the typical emulation-of-patterns type of approach.

Instead of trying to correct the flaws directly, it is better to try to correct and refine the concepts and satisfactions of the hit. The basic flaws, which fit in well only with habits of their own kind, will then ordinarily be diminished correspondingly. The compensations and coercions generated by those flaws will lose their meaning and appeal, and will tend to disappear also.

Notes on

chapter six
follow-through

One of the elements of a stroke most intimately related to the contact interval is the follow-through. The close relationship comes about because the acceleration of the racquet necessary to maximize the length of the contact interval is the major factor in determining the nature of the follow-through.

But it must seem strange to the reader that we already turn to the tag end of a stroke, by which time the business part has ended, without first having discussed all of the components of a swing in a more logical sequence. The explanation offered is that the purpose of this book is not to develop or justify certain patterns or techniques, or to discredit any of them either for that matter. The goal is to create the understandings that can be used to mold and improve the patterns of choice by a better and more complete exploitation of the characteristics of elasticity.

An arrangement of topics that provides for an early discussion of the mechanics of a hit seems to be the most efficient way to develop the understandings needed to begin the progress toward the higher levels of play. The importance of those understandings is not dependant on adherence to a particular style. It is not necessary, for instance, to employ a specific stance or grip before it becomes possible to begin to apply the already discussed concepts of elasticity, visualizations, illusions, and compensations to whatever techniques the reader happens to be using at the moment.

ORIGINS AND FUNCTIONS OF FOLLOW-THROUGH

The interval of contact was previously discussed in some detail, and was described as the only part of the stroke that had any direct effect on the behavior of the ball. However this should not be taken to suggest that a person can feel free to do anything at all in either the preparation or the follow-through. What happens before contact should produce or lead up to what should happen during, and what happens after is the natural consequence of both. The hit, whether done rightly or wrongly, thus depends on the preparation, and both largely determine the follow-through.

The ball is constantly gaining velocity even during the latter part of contact, and hence is moving fastest just after contact ends. Accelerating the racquet to try to have it keep up with the ball increases the tendency of the racquet to overshoot the mark and extend the follow-through.

Conversely, if there is no acceleration into the follow-through the racquet is almost certain to be slowing down during contact. For instance, even a constant forward momentum of the racquet diminished by the momentum of the ball at impact translates into a slowing down of the racquet. This creates an inefficiency in both the storage and recovery of energies.

The real follow-through cannot directly affect the ball because it starts when contact is broken. It is therefore not an end in itself, but is significant only in so far as an improper ending either reflects back into the hit or is a result of improper execution during the hit. Whatever beneficial activities occur during contact cannot start or end in that very short period of time, and neither can the undesirable. So an idiosyncrasy during follow-through, when it doesn't matter, may very well have existed, been started, or at least been prepared for during or before contact, when it most certainly does matter.

Some follow-through is good, but only in the sense that it is the product of proper racquet momentum and acceleration. Making the racquet travel according to a pattern, or finish at a prescribed end point, will not automatically optimize whatever benefits are presumed to be derived therefrom. Follow-through has the passive function of providing an easy and natural finish to a well executed swing, and that is all. It is neither a means to an end nor a path to a cure. However it can have significance as a symptom of various other types of problems, such as deficient acceleration, improper timing, circular swing, and inappropriate hitting point.

DEFINING THE END POINT OF THE SWING

The classic ending of a ground stroke has ordinarily been defined as having the racquet head, or the front edge of it, point in the direction of the hit. But that rule is too restrictive and unnatural for those players who do not need to observe exaggerated requirements in the follow-through to control harmful tendencies in the swing. Trying to finish with the racquet in a prescribed position also has the adverse effect of focusing attention on a nonfunctional detail that in itself does not deserve any direct attention.

In subtle ways the preoccupation with an intended ending may interfere with the more useful and functional elements of a swing. As long as the hit is proper the player ought to be free to have the racquet end up as occurs naturally and takes the least effort, attention, and time, whether that end position can be defined as orthodox or not. Where the racquet starts from is more important than where it finishes. Also, it may be unfair to ask novices to subscribe to theories concerning a stylized ending that the pros themselves do not use and would find burdensome and counterproductive.

However the player should also be aware of the dangers inherent in not keeping the racquet moving in a consistently forward direction during contact. Any attempt to change the racquet heading or its speed too soon after contact may result in those changes being actually initiated during contact, with undesirable effects on the processes that are proceeding therein.

THE SHORT AND THE LONG

Many people with deficient follow-through think that they understand how long it should be, and that they fully observe the requirements. But the execution is almost always considerably less extensive than the intentions, and unfortunately the intentions may quite often not be based on an adequate knowledge of the principles involved. To inexpert players carrying the racquet forward to anything approaching the adequate will in all likelihood feel highly exaggerated, something to be tolerated in practice under the eye of the coach but not to be risked in actual play with a point at stake.

There is greater harm in cutting contact short than in continuing the follow-through too long. In view of this danger some overemphasis on follow-through, as is fairly common when coaches demonstrate the standard patterns, probably amounts to being in error on the safe side. However, extending the follow-through too far can be a disadvantage too, as will be shown.

THE PROBLEM OF THE POSE

Some players, especially those with "schooled" strokes, compound the problem of prematurely curtailing the swing by then paradoxically holding the end position too long. This is discrimination against what is useful in favor of what is mere display, with the double penalty of both compromising the contact interval and also delaying the start of the preparation for the next shot.

Although some people hold the end position too long most do the opposite: start to get ready for the next shot before sufficiently satisfying the requirements of the present. It is therefore risky policy to advise players who already do not carry the swing far enough that an extended follow-through is a luxury in which it may be unwise to indulge.

If the finish of the current swing is not satisfactory there will be penalties in terms of accuracy and effectiveness. But if more time than advisable is spent on the termination of the current stroke then the ball had better be put away because the opponent has been given a lot of extra time to do the same. There may not be a need to worry about a next swing. It is therefore sometimes advisable to compromise between the valid needs of the conflicting considerations, usually by taking a little off both the follow-through of the present shot and the preparation for the next.

Either choice may weaken a player's strokes, and the opponent may then be able to come on all the more strong. At the expert level any weakness is likely to be taken advantage of, and any slight unpreparedness for a return apt to be noticed and exploited. A player must not only be ready but must be ready for any type of return, and the one for which there is the least readiness is the one most likely to come along. Therefor, the compromises to the follow-through that have to be made as expedients should not be continued when the pressure is less severe and there is time to use more optimum preparation and execution.

THE URGE TO STOP SHORT

When there is a feeling that a stroke will be difficult to control, or that an error absolutely cannot be afforded at the moment, the player may try to stop the racquet short due to a fear that the ball will be misdirected, and that using a normal follow-through will only increase the probability and amplify the seriousness. But stopping the racquet short has adverse effects on the storage and recovery of energy, and on both the direction and spin of the ball. Although the ball will not then have the speed to go very far astray there will be an increased probability that it will go astray.

A means of making some use of the fear of hitting out freely is to consider the fear as an indication that the subconscious mind may have recognized a flaw, and that it is important enough so that the follow-through has to be compromised. This sets up the situation, as discussed in the chapter on "compensations," where there is a double chance of improvement: successfully replace the flaw and then the related compromises can be discarded also.

Two other reasons why players may cut the follow-through short are for one that they simply don't understand the nature of the contact interval and the role of the follow-through, and for the other that a quick termination of the swing equates in the mind to a quick flight of the ball to its destination. The latter idea is quite at odds with reality. Unless such perceptions can be overcome via acquaintance with the nature of the contact interval and the function of follow-through the undesirable mannerisms will likely continue to be unremovable.

THE EXAMPLE OF THE PROS

A common misconception is that the pros cut their follow-through short too. Sometimes they do, but careful observation will reveal that an adequate acceleration of the racquet through contact is generally observed, and only then does the forward travel of the racquet end, perhaps with some abruptness. The forward momentum of the racquet is not particularly easy to overcome, and the experts do not waste undue energy trying to stop it. On ground strokes they tend to accomplish the purpose by changing the racquet's direction since this can be done with less effort than is required to stop the motion entirely.

Casual viewers, while perhaps noting that the end of the stroke may not resemble a traditional follow-through, are generally not similarly observant of the behavior of the racquet during contact. They may thus mistakenly attribute to the business part of the stroke the characteristics that pertain mostly to what happened after contact had ended. Observation of just the forward motion of the racquet will usually reveal that even when the expert players show some signs of stopping or diverting it too quickly they nevertheless have by that time carried it through much further than do the players at lower levels.

While the pros cannot allow more than minor compromises in the functional elements of a stroke they are under intense pressure to be ready for the next shot. They are therefore just as careful to avoid using any excess of style in the follow-through as they are to make sure of getting just as much as possible out of contact. This is evidenced by their ability to hit with heavy pace and still almost always move in an unhurried manner to an ideal spot to get properly ready for the return.

After all the emphasis that has been placed on an adequate follow-through obtained by continuing the acceleration of the racquet through contact, one standard precaution is in order: not to overdo it. Forcing the racquet to continue the follow-through further than necessary will provide diminishing returns in the amount of additional pace on the ball, and may introduce unnaturalness, a loss of balance, the use of excess effort, and a lack of readiness for the next shot. The acceleration should start slowly, be slight, steady, and unforced; not violent, sudden, and artificial. Doing whatever is required for an optimum hit will insure that too much will not be made of a nonfunctional element such as follow-through.

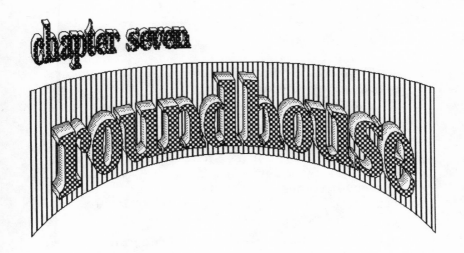

chapter seven
roundhouse

The slowing or even stopping of the racquet have already been mentioned as habits that make for an inefficient contact interval. A means of slowing the forward movement that is ordinarily not recognized as such is roundhouse: swinging the racquet in a curved path around the body rather than forward in the direction of the hit. Even some top players appear to use roundhouse, although for the most part the appearances are deceiving. They generally do not allow the curved termination of the swing to intrude on the contact interval to a significant degree, except perhaps when they succumb to emotions or pressure or are not playing too well.

THE COMPONENTS OF MOTION

The horizontal motion of the racquet in a ground stroke can be described as being made up of two components at right angles to each other: forward and sideward. When the racquet is moving forward the sideward component is zero. The sideward move is quite large when it is introduced deliberately for the purpose of side spin. But even in a properly executed ground stroke the forward component diminishes rapidly and the sideward becomes correspondingly larger very soon after the racquet goes past the hitting point.

If this deviation occurs a little earlier so as to intrude on contact it reduces forward racquet motion and resultant ball velocity just as effectively as if the swing were simply slowed down or stopped. As the forward component becomes smaller the ability of the racquet to keep up with the accelerating ball deteriorates, and the ball then goes quickly out of contact.

When roundhouse is present the moment to moment horizontal attitude and horizontal direction of motion of the racquet are somewhat indeterminate, and to a lesser extent so also are the vertical. Control can be very erratic and the path of the ball hard to predict. Roundhouse is therefore likely to result in a powerless, unreliable hit.

A player confronted with these consequences is likely to react to the disappointing speed of the ball by hitting ever more compulsively, which in turn will further accentuate the roundhouse and its effects. Violent exertions seldom solve any problems or confer any benefits, but are pretty sure to aggravate old troubles and create some that are new.

THE ORIGINS OF ROUNDHOUSE

Roundhouse is one of the most prevalent of faults. It can be a serious problem even in strokes where it would seem that there is little likelihood that it will occur, such as the serve and even the volley. The effects there will be discussed more completely in the chapter on the "SERVE."

The flaw is difficult to cure because it has a multitude of origins, and usually in combination: using a too pronounced body turn, turning too soon to get ready for the next shot, turning to watch the other side of the court or the path of the ball, moving the front foot back or the back foot forward during the swing, jumping in a circular manner, using a swing incompatible with the stance, not shifting the body forward into the shot, pulling the body backward, holding the arm stiff and swinging the racquet by rotating the body, trying to move the racquet with a greater speed than the strength of the arm is capable of achieving, pulling the elbow in, not understanding the nature of a hit or the requirements of the contact interval, swinging in a tired or lazy manner, etc.

If the arm is held out too far, as when extended for a ball that is almost beyond reach, the arm and shoulder cannot straighten the arc of the swing on the approach to the hitting point. The racquet is therefore forced to travel in somewhat of a circle in that vicinity. At the other extreme, when the racquet is held in too close to the body, it travels in a tight circle and veers rapidly toward the side after the midpoint of the swing. This results in an insignificant forward component of velocity in the hitting zone.

Roundhouse can also be caused by swinging too soon for such reasons as poor timing, excessively emotional execution, and making up for lost time due to late preparation, or for a late start of the forward swing. There can even be situations where some types of roundhouse occur because they are mistakenly assumed to be embellishments that abet a good swing.

For instance, an apparently harmless or even decorative sideways flourish of the racquet at the end of the forehand swing may actually amount to roundhouse during contact. The player can become fully aware of say a lack of power on the forehand without having a remote inkling that the cherished pleasant flourish at the end, instead of being a stylish and rhythmic enhancement, is just roundhouse in disguise.

It is easier to fall into the habit of hitting roundhouse from an open stance than from a closed. But quite a number of expert players, even at the tournament level, hit forehands from a fairly open stance and yet do not generally hit roundhouse. The hitting point, timing, development of racquet momentum, etc., have to be just about optimum to hit well from that position, and some extra strength of the arm is also required. For the latter reason women players tend not to hit from a true open stance as much as men. On the backhand roundhouse is very difficult to avoid if the stance is at all open.

ALSO IN BASEBALL

In baseball, as could be expected with the much heavier bat used and the suddenness of the swing, the players there are even less likely to succeed than in tennis in having the bat travel almost entirely in the direction of the hit during contact. A roundhouse swing is therefore more common in baseball than in tennis, even at the professional level.

Occasionally the bat is swung around with all the violent effort that the player can muster, sometimes to the extent that the trunk of the body is noticeably retreating backward as the bat goes forward. This is a violation of the principles of hitting, and unfortunately not only are the elastic processes the same as in tennis but so also are the penalties that go with improper execution.

REMEDY THE CAUSE

The task in obtaining a cure for roundhouse is formidable. It is first necessary to learn to feel whether or not roundhouse is present. This is not at all easy because it is notably difficult for people to visualize their own habits, and because the problem often occurs only for a brief instant late in the stroke when the attention can have been switched to the other court. Although roundhouse in the late stages of the swing may not be easy to detect it probably will still have grossly detrimental effects on the shot.

For a cure it is particularly useful to think in terms of having the body become totally involved in getting ready for a solid hit, since if roundhouse is present the body is almost undoubtedly being prepared for roundhouse, not for a proper forward swing. So committing the body early and using the correct intents will make it less likely that there will be a switch to roundhouse later on. In fact, getting completely prepared for a good hit will help in suppressing many other types of bad habits as well.

It should be noted that in the list of suggestions above it is not being recommended that the player should merely be told to straighten out the swing. People seldom deliberately use a circular swing so they can't deliberately discontinue it. Roundhouse is a result, not a cause, and it is always the cause that has to be rooted out before it is possible to get rid of the result. The progress can be enhanced if the player has a working knowledge of what constitutes a good hit and is aware of the nature of roundhouse, and can therefore identify probable causes.

Although the normal rotation of the body can deteriorate into roundhouse some rotation has to be present for naturalness, as well as to augment the free movement of the arm and assist in the forward acceleration of the racquet. Body rotation is needed toward the end of the swing on the forehand to move the body and shoulder out of the way of the arm. Hitting with no participation rotation-wise by the body can be just as bad as hitting with too much.

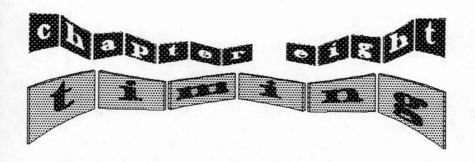

Although there are widely different styles of stroke production all have the common requirement of good timing. The term signifies much more than just meeting the ball at the most appropriate hitting point. In good timing all the functional elements of a stroke, from the details of getting into position to the nature of the follow-through, are each sequenced and optimized with great precision within the pattern of the stroke. The actual hit will be adversely affected if any of the prior elements are not readied, started, interleaved, developed, and ended satisfactorily and at the precisely right times.

If any element is mistimed then the essential initial conditions for the succeeding elements may not be set up properly. And in addition those latter elements may be handicapped in fulfilling their individual functions by being squeezed out of their proper sequence and made to start either too late or too soon. This is evident in the uncoordinated appearance of the strokes of unskilled players, even when the racquet arrives at the exactly correct hitting point at the right time.

TYPES OF TIMING

There are two types of timing, internal and external. Internal timing is involved with just the mechanics of the swing and the hit, while the external is concerned with the coordination of the swing with the arrival of the ball. In an ideal sense external timing should not be permitted to have any direct influence on stroke production or on the internal timing, but should rather just allow them to happen unhindered in any way.

In other words, the player should anticipate and allow for the external circumstances so well that the internal timing can be carried out as if unrelated to anything except the mechanics of the hit. Such complete separation is only theoretically possible since nobody is capable of perfect internal or external timing. The internal timing must therefore often get involved with adjustments for deficiencies in the external, and vice versa.

The various elements that must be timed in proper sequence are as diverse as the start of the backswing, transfer of weight, turn of the shoulders, flex of the wrist, and the development of racquet momentum. Correcting internal timing problems is difficult because it is not often possible to directly observe and isolate bad timing of particular individual internal elements. The relationships to the external timing, to the overall results, and to other aspects of the stroke are even more difficult to establish.

The player can control the hitting point quite effectively by moving around the court as needed. But the ball could still be to the side, high, or low, or whatever, and the stroke is thereby required to be a backhand, forehand, overhead, etc. No matter what the stroke and the height of the ball, it should be possible to time the internal elements as if the swing were entirely independent of external conditions.

THE SWING-CONTROLLED STROKE

There is an old adage that says that in a correct serve there is a toss at the swing rather than a swing at the toss. In other words, the server should feel free to use an ideal swing to carry the racquet through an ideal hitting point since there should be a reasonable certainty that the ball can also be made to appear at about that same point at about the right instant.

If the ball is not normally at the optimum hitting point when the racquet gets there then the ideal swing should not be compromised to meet the ball wherever else it may customarily be. The timing of the toss, the toss itself, or both should be modified until the ball does appear as expected. This is discussed more fully in the chapter on the "SERVE."

For strokes other than the serve "tossing at the swing" is a little difficult because the "toss" is made by the opponent. However the point of impact is controlled by the receiver through the external timing of the swing. If the receiver carries out the preparation and the external timing in an exemplary enough manner to make it possible to use an ideal swing, then it will be as if the racquet just happened to meet the ball when both arrived at the perfect hitting point at the same time.

There should be no intrusion of push, paw, poke, pull, jerk, slap, swipe, roundhouse, slowing, stopping, hurrying, leaning, cramping, reaching, or other manipulations and compensations that detract from the hit. If such expedients are allowed to occur then the timing that is used will not be compatible with any but the individual collection of bad habits involved, and specifically not with a proper "swing-controlled" stroke. The bad timing and bad swing each needs and deserves the other, and neither can be discarded independently because each depends on the presence of the other.

A paradoxical but rather common obstacle to improvement for many players is that they often interpret the more unpleasant and jarring sensations associated with improper timing as indicative of a very hard hit. Even top players are apt to succumb to this misconception and sometimes allow an urge to hit hard cause a regression to habits relating back to their amateurish days.

TIMING INTERACTIONS

When a change is made in the pattern of a stroke the assimilation problems generally turn out to be very difficult because of the complexity and interaction of the internal and external timing, and also because of problems of compatibility of the new features with those that are retained. Both the timing and the execution of each retained element tend to remain unchanged in spite of the need to adjust to the new elements in the swing.

With such interaction of factors no wonder that good timing may seem to be mostly a natural endowment rather than an acquired skill. But if just average athletic ability is combined with a rational intent for the hit, and with a fair understanding of such basic factors as preparation, momentum, roundhouse, follow-through, etc., then the ordinary timing problems can be corrected to a substantial degree. At higher levels of skill there is little violation of the basic principles, so the amount of possible improvement may not be very much. But each small increment of improvement there gets to be of disproportionate importance.

VARIATION IN RACQUET ATTITUDE

Ground strokes have sometimes been claimed to involve an exactly perpendicular attitude of the racquet face during at least the latter part of the forward swing. If this were true there would then be the substantial advantage of not having to be concerned with the timing of the changes in the attitude of the racquet during the swing. But the current trend away from the strictly classical style, and the rise in popularity of the heavy topspin shot with the Western forehand grip, make variation in the attitude of the racquet not just permissible but necessary in many strokes.

Whatever may be the recommendations for the racquet attitude at the hit, it is now generally admitted that perpendicularity does not exist throughout the stroke. So hitting point variations affect the attitude at various stages of the swing. A full discussion of racquet attitude is left for the chapter on that subject.

TIMING THE BACKSWING

A significant but unnecessary problem is the timing of the backswing. A common mistake is to keep the racquet pointing forward until the ball has approached so close as not to allow getting the racquet back soon enough for a normal forward swing. This delay amounts to timing the backswing, instead of the forward swing, with the bounce of the ball. The resultant problems are bound to plague the remainder of the stroke.

A late backswing can affect the whole character of a swing, including the development of momentum, the extent of reinforcement, the amount of reserve strength, the degree of extension of the arm, etc. But instead of trying to avoid the lateness by thinking in terms of the familiar phrase "racquet back" it is better to visualize getting the whole body involved and prepared for the hit. The detail of "racquet back" will then take care of itself.

A more specific means of improving the timing of the backswing is to think in terms of being ready to begin to develop the forward racquet momentum by about the time the ball bounces. If it is necessary to consciously focus on a single aspect of timing it probably should be the timing of the development of racquet momentum. The backswing must not be allowed to interfere with that development.

CAN'T BE PERFECT

"Perfect" timing of all elements is not even theoretically attainable because there is some incompatibility between the needs of the various elements, between racquet velocity and hitting point for instance. If the racquet is continually accelerated during contact, as it should be, maximum racquet velocity is obtained not at the hitting point but a little after contact has ended.

A lack of understanding of this particular concept generates an intent to maximize the racquet velocity just at the beginning of contact, or even a little before, instead of a little after. This habit is responsible for many fundamentally wrong strokes. The impact then tends to be an anticlimax, resembling a glancing slap rather than a solid hit. Another factor that becomes optimized in an area further out in front than the hitting point is reinforcement. This is covered in the next chapter.

Optimum overall timing is merely the best possible compromise of the timing needs of all the individual elements of a stroke. The correct balance is determined by the feel in the context of the best use of momentum and the most solid hit that can be obtained with a sustainable amount of effort.

CONSEQUENCES OF BAD TIMING

If the swing is late (ball approaches too close) there will be a feeling of the arm getting caught in a position where it has insufficient strength, of the racquet not having developed enough momentum, and of the ball creating a heavy and perhaps painful shock at impact. The player becomes increasingly aware of the lack of time as the ball approaches closer, prompting an attempt to hurry the racquet by pulling the elbow in toward the body.

This is an instinctive reaction to provide extra strength as a substitute for missing momentum, as well as to shorten the swing interval by shortening the length of the arc. An elbow that is habitually brought in very close may thus be merely a symptom of lateness in the preparation or in the start of the forward swing.

If a player is too early with the swing (the ball hasn't approached close enough at the hit) the problem becomes one of a lack of reach instead of time, and a different collection of compensations is in order. One compensation is to push the racquet through the too far out in front hitting point, rather than swinging through a more comfortably reachable location. On an early hit the racquet is getting to be at the extremity of its travel where it begins to go into roundhouse. So the push is used to substitute force for momentum in an attempt to continue to move the racquet in the desired forward direction.

In this situation there are at least three interacting problems to overcome: the too early completion of most of the swing, the push, and a too far out in front hitting point. It can be seen that merely trying to change any one by itself has little chance of success. One possible approach to a solution would be an attempt to determine the rationale for the quick or just early swing.

Since the push will not provide adequate pace the player is likely to try the remedy of swinging even faster than before. But the extra effort will bring the racquet around even sooner than previously, further aggravating the problem of the too early arrival of the racquet at the location of the preferred hitting point. Consequently, with the instinctive remedies tending to aggravate the situation, people who are in the habit of hitting early may get to believe that correct timing and a satisfactory pace are skills that are not within their capabilities for reasons beyond comprehension and control.

Some players may use a slap instead of a push for similar reasons and with similar effect. The push and the slap are deficient in pace because of inadequate racquet momentum, lack of the necessary acceleration through contact, and a cutting down on the contact interval. The slap has additional drawbacks in that the racquet quickly begins to go around instead of forward, and in that it is an arm alone swing and thus isolates the weight of the body from participation in the hit.

THE CHOICE BETWEEN EARLY OR LATE

The choices available to a player as to the location of the hitting point are not just in terms of negatives, since hitting either early or late has its positive side. In order to be able to make intelligent decisions about where to shift the hitting point, so that particular aspects of the stroke can be improved or certain problems minimized, a player should have some knowledge of the alternatives.

The major advantages of hitting a ball late (ball approaches closer than normal) are:

There is considerable remaining room for forward arm travel available at contact. For that reason the acceleration and follow-through can proceed without restraint.

There is a large leeway in the hitting zone, which eases the timing problems compared with the situation when hitting early.

The racquet path is more easily kept to a rather straight line through and past contact.

On forehands the body has less of a tendency to be in the way of the arm in the latter part of the swing.

The stance is not apt to get to be too open.

The movement of the body and the shoulder into the shot is not almost all used up before the hit occurs.

The wrist does not have to be bent back at the hit to face the racquet in the desired direction.

On backhands it is easier to hit topspin if the hitting point is not too far out in front.

The major advantages of hitting early (the ball not yet having arrived at the normal hitting point) are:

There is a longer swing in which to develop racquet momentum.

The arm is far enough forward so that it is angled slightly toward the line of flight of the ball (rather than being more nearly at right angles with that line), and for that reason gives better reinforcement with the body.

A ball out in front appears to have less than its actual speed, making it easier to follow and judge.

It is easy to keep the ball and the opponent in the field of vision.

In reaching out at the end of the swing the body is pulled around to face the net, facilitating getting into position and being ready for the opponent's return.

NARROW VIEWS OF TIMING

Associating timing with just one item is overemphasis of that one element at the expense of the many others associated with the very complex timing process. Therefore the act of paying increased attention to a single detail when one's strokes are not working properly is more likely to result in deterioration than in improvement.

Changing the timing of the elements in a stroke can result in a change in the hitting point. But just correcting the hitting point will not automatically improve on bad internal timing. The hitting point can be entirely correct while the internal timing can be decidedly not so. For that reason a new hitting point will not be retained unless the customary good or bad timing of the internal elements and the development of racquet momentum is made compatible with that hitting point.

Merely knowing during a match that the timing is off is gratuitous information, providing more in the way of worry than hope in the way of improvement. Even subsequent heavy drill on a specific faulty element, such as the location of the hitting point, is not apt to be of much help. The interrelated circumstances have to be addressed, and perhaps the only genuinely safe way is to improve on the concepts and the execution of the hit and the satisfactions involved. There is more on this topic in the chapter "WATCHING THE BALL."

THE SOURCES OF TIMING VARIATIONS

An episode regularly seen even in tournaments is a player mis-hitting the ball and then expressing frustration by action or attitude as if to suggest that the equipment is guilty of behavior so perverse as to be beyond understanding or tolerance. But the equipment is hardly capable of momentary lapses in performance and of a magnitude to be visibly evident in the results, to say nothing of accounting for a grossly misdirected ball.

The most common causes of errors lie in the timing, but as has just been explained this covers a large area. The well known description of tennis as a game of inches could more correctly be in reference to ten-thousandths of a second. A further examination into the generally overlooked intricacies where many timing problems really lie is therefore in order. In most cases it may not be possible to correct for the specific miniscule timing variations involved, but the mere awareness of their existence tends, over a period of time, to introduce all the correction needed.

HOLDING BACK

An error that players are often guilty of is to hold back on the follow-through at critical moments in a match, and this action will almost always commence before contact. The slowing down of the racquet has a secondary consequence of which the player is not likely to be aware: the hit will be a little late (the ball approaches a little closer than usual). The lateness in the timing is made more severe by the fact that the racquet should normally be accelerating through contact rather than slowing down.

The opposite condition is also a source of variations in the hitting point: timing being advanced too much.

The most obvious way of advancing timing is by simply swinging faster than usual. This is typically made to occur by bringing the elbow inward so as to swing the racquet through a smaller than usual arc, and with a vicious application of energy.

When a timing variation occurs in either the late or early direction, and the errors begin to mount, there is then further excuse to get more cautious in the one case and to swing more intemperately in the other, merely aggravating the respective timing problems. So at critical times there often is both a frustrating loss of pace and also a seemingly mysterious surge of timing errors. In such situations it is incorrect to say "my timing was off." What should be said is something like "I got chicken (or reckless) and changed the length and speed of my strokes, but didn't realize that this made a difference in the timing."

INTERNAL AND EXTERNAL TIMING SUBTLETIES

Earliness or lateness is generally considered to refer to the arrival of the racquet in relation to that of the ball. However the motions of the arm and the body may be early or late with respect to each other too. Although in many cases the location of the hitting point is the visible evidence of a problem with timing, a lack of coordination of the movements of the arm and body also constitutes improper timing. Instead of making an effort to discover and correct the real flaws responsible for the nature of the execution or the location of the hitting point the player is apt to exclaim "WATCH THE BALL!!!"

Complicating the picture is the fact that some types of changes in the patterns of strokes affect timing in ways that may seem to be the reverse of what should happen. For instance, exaggerating the step into a shot equates to retarded external timing rather than advanced. This comes about because the forward move of the body brings the racquet into contact with the ball sooner than without the movement, and therefore the arm has not had a chance to finish its customary sequence of actions and reach its standard position with respect to the body at the hit. This phenomena is discussed further in the chapter on "BLASTING."

The rotation of the body can cause either advanced or retarded timing. If the rotation brings the racquet around faster than usual then the external timing is advanced. However, if the body rotates ahead and drags the arm along behind then the timing is likely to be retarded, externally as well as internally. While this line of reasoning may seem obvious to some people the trouble is that very few people have thought about it enough to take it into consideration during play, especially on critical points when there are more compelling demands on the attention.

The real timing complications will almost always be much more complicated than as discussed above, and will involve many other factors: the bend of the arm and wrist, tightness of grip, attitude of racquet, shift of weight, etc. If an accurate enough analysis, or effective experimentation, cannot be made at the time of the hit then about the only safe recourse for the time being is to avoid the action that caused the difficulty. That is much better than repeatedly using a technique that repeatedly causes the same error, perhaps also causing the player's game to fall apart.

DECEPTIVE SPEED OF THE BALL

An oncoming ball appears to move faster as it approaches closer, and therefore becomes progressively harder to watch as it nears the hitting zone. Usually there is not apt to be conscious recognition of this factor as such. However the effect is experienced often enough so that over a period of time most players begin to adjust by moving the hitting point forward from the optimum for more convenience in viewing. Although there may then be a sense of security in terms of seeing the ball more clearly there is likely to be a deterioration in respect to the effectiveness and accuracy of the hit.

A similar accommodation often occurs when taking a ball that lands short. It is quite common for players of all levels to hit too early at a low ball by reaching out with the racquet way ahead of the standard hitting point. One justification, of course, is to try to hit the ball before it touches the ground again.

It so happens in the case of low balls that hitting just a little early is not at all wrong, since for low bounces the body can and should be leaning forward a little more than usual, and this moves the shoulder forward to a similar extent. Generally speaking, the correct hitting point is determined in relation to the hitting shoulder, not the "net" foot (closest to the net when in a sideways stance). But for most strokes the foot happens to be a more convenient reference point for purposes of instruction.

HITTING ON THE MOVE

A disadvantage associated with moving up for a hit is that the ball is hard to see for a player in motion. The problem is aggravated by the fact that running forward in effect increases the speed of the ball. So if a normal swing is used while running in then the hit will tend to be a little late, ball approaches too close. The ball will then go wide on the same side as the racquet except where the player anticipates and compensates, or panics and overcompensates.

The standard wisdom is not to hit on the run but to first stop and then hit, and this may be a reasonable precaution. But if it is necessary to take the ball while running in on it, as is quite common, the swing must either be a little faster or be started a miniscule moment earlier than usual because the time available to get the racquet around will have been reduced.

The reverse of the above reasoning is applicable to hits that have to be made while retreating from the oncoming ball. In this situation the pace of the ball is effectively slowed. With a normal swing the racquet has more than the usual amount of time to complete its journey. So it arrives at the best location for the hitting point before the ball gets there. A temporary cure is to swing a little slower or start the forward swing a little later. The real cure is to improve on the concepts of the hit. Another solution is to try to always get back soon enough so as to be able to stop and step into the hit normally.

When making a desperate run toward either side it is usually best not to change the timing from that used for a normal, easy swing. But here an overcompensation with a quick swing seems to be the rule, and the ball is usually hit too early, even in those cases where preparation is late, which is also usual. In addition, there is a tendency to hold back on the follow-through. All this makes for an unpredictable, ineffective hit when such consequences are least tolerable.

As all tennis players know, it is very difficult to maintain optimum techniques and timing when under pressure. But some of this is due to abandonment of the regular game rather than inherent difficulty. For instance, when making a shot on the run there often is an ordinarily unnoticed flaw of not making a preparatory body turn. This in itself is enough to ruin a shot. If you don't have an idea of the respects in which your techniques and timing are likely to be off in such situations, and are unaware of the types of adjustments that can be of help, you have small chance of recovering composure and making corrections.

VARIATIONS IN THE BOUNCE

Inexpert players often neglect to make timing adjustments for the nature of the bounce. Besides the factor of the height there is also the matter of the rebound angle off the court. The angle of the bounce tends to be equal to the angle of the impact except as influenced by spin, wind, and the amount of friction inherent between the ball and the court surface. The greater the angle of impact with the ground (closer to vertical) the more necessary is it to move in to obtain a customary hit at a customary hitting point. The tendency is not to move in far enough and then compensate by swinging faster and reaching forward with the racquet.

On a high bounce the forward component of the speed of the ball is low, and this circumstance requires the receiver to introduce a corresponding timing delay in the forward swing. The receiver has to generate most of the pace on such returns, and this takes a good swing with plenty of acceleration and follow-through. The extra vigor shortens the interval of the swing, creating a need for an additional delay in the timing. Many errors can result from not changing the timing to suit the requirements of the situation. So bad hits off easy bounces are very common for good reason.

TIMING THE BACKHAND

It is not generally realized that the timing for the backhand is somewhat different from that for the forehand, mainly because the backhand involves a bigger arc and a slightly more forward hitting point in the case of the classic patterns. This timing variance accounts for some of the extraordinary difficulty that many players have with that shot. The matter is discussed in greater length in the chapter on the "BACKHAND."

DIFFICULTY OF ISOLATING TIMING PROBLEMS

Timing has to be applied to many supplementary actions, such as the involvement of the feet, body, and shoulder. Maybe the rotation or movement of the body occurred too soon, or perhaps the front foot was put into position too early, rather than that the swing of the racquet was mistimed. It is impractical to analyze and discuss each of the many possible problems separately. In general they will be automatically corrected and refined as the concepts and the feel of the hit are improved.

Where this is not enough to eliminate a timing problem it may still be possible to isolate the error and work out a solution. At this point in the book the reader should have acquired a sufficient knowledge of the principles involved in stroke production so that special individual problems can be investigated with some success. Slow motion visualization (SMV) can be of help. Another device is to reenact a faulty technique several times in all its poor form so that the repeated unpleasant experience may both pinpoint the source and help motivate a reform. As mentioned several times, the ability to learn is a skill to be mastered the same as any other tennis skill.

TIMING AS A TACTIC

Although timing can be used as a principal element of strategy by occasionally changing the behavior of the ball so as to cause the opponent to mistime and mishit, this should only be done during play and not during the pre-game warm-up. The latter is a cooperative effort by the players to get their timing under control before play begins.

During the warm-up it is strictly unethical for either player to run the other around, hit poor bounces, or try in other ways to unsettle the opponent's timing or composure. Even during play the techniques for tricking an opponent to mistime a shot should be confined to variation in speed, bounce, depth, spin, etc., without resort to behavior designed to upset timing, composure, and concentration.

chapter nine

involvement of the body

It is very difficult to describe more than a few of the elements involved in the preparation and execution of a proper swing for just one type of stroke in just one style: the movements of the feet, knees, hips, shoulders, wrist, etc.; which muscles to tense and relax, how, when, and why; the coordination with the arrival of the ball; etc. And such explanations would not do much good since execution varies with the player, objective, and circumstance. However, since the hit and some of the intricacies of timing have been defined, it is now desirable and possible to consider a few of the aspects of the involvement of the body.

NOT BY ARM ALONE

Even when the timing, acceleration, hitting point and all the rest seem to be satisfactory there is still the danger of unknowingly harboring several other deficiencies. One of the most important and prevalent of these is allowing the arm to do the work alone without reinforcement from the body. Under that circumstance the jolt of the ball can negate enough momentum of the racquet to seriously impair the storage and recovery of energy.

Many players are not aware of that fact. So to them it is not at all apparent why it should be necessary to make extensive use of the body just to swing the arm and a rather light racquet with the purpose of hitting a small, light ball. They see nothing in the nature of the task to justify the idea that reinforcement of the arm with the body is critical to efficient recovery of energy from the elasticities.

The failure of the body to take part in the swing is frequently a distinguishing characteristic between a "schooled" stroke and one that may be somewhat strange style-wise because of having been self taught, but one that can nevertheless be said to have great effectiveness and naturalness because of having active participation by the body. Unless the body gets involved the real essence of a stroke is simply not there, no matter that otherwise there may be considerable resemblance to the classic or other excellent form.

The "arm-alone" swing is largely due to three flaws in execution: (1) a too passive role for the body, (2) poorly timed use, or (3) over zealous involvement. These major causes of failure to attain a suitable cooperation between arm and body stem from a variety of more basic causes, such as over cautiousness, emotional execution, and ignorance about the requirements for the contact interval. In most cases the fact of the body being out of sync with the arm will be easily detectable in itself, but in its more subtle forms the flaw may make its presence known only through such symptoms as an unpleasant feel to the hit and a lack of pace on the ball.

HALF-WAY INVOLVEMENT

Even when the body gets properly prepared there may not be a good use of it due to the player switching from a good preparation involving the body to a bad execution depending on the arm alone. A veneer of style is superimposed over the preparation and backswing, but a clumsily executed forward swing, hit, and follow-through then ensue.

A humorous and very common example is in the serves of quite a few recreational players. The start is made with what seems to be strong purpose and an impressive buildup, but this is followed by a swivel of the body toward the net and a restrained tap with the racquet to send a soft pop shot in the direction of the service court. A more complete discussion of this particular problem is given in a subsequent chapter on the "SERVE."

Without trying to be funny, it is useful to note that mothers quickly learn without instruction how to deliver a meaningful whack to the underside of a misbehaving child. Yet some of those same mothers may manage to acquire only a very diffident "arm-alone" forehand even though having had tennis lessons from the best instructors around.

The difference is largely due to intent. In applying physical persuasion to a child the very whole-hearted intent is to deliver a properly weighty message, whereas with the forehand the intent is often just to act out what is usually an inaccurate interpretation of a highly sketchy outline of a very complicated sequence of events. The body must get into the act of swinging the racquet so that the ball will also get a properly weighty message.

PREPARATION DETERMINES RESULT

To a considerable extent a good or bad shot is the result of the corresponding type of preparation. Knowingly or not, players make the choice as to the result fairly early. The bad shot is generally the unwanted but yet natural result of a preparation inadvertently designed for that specific purpose. The type of preparation of the body that occurs before a poor shot is as exactly appropriate for that result as the preparation before a good shot is equally as appropriate for that outcome. Hence, getting the body suitably ready for a weighty shot is a very important part of developing significant momentum in the ball. It is not an add-on feature.

The commonly heard advice relating to preparation such as "turn," "step," and "racquet back" may work well for the initial lessons for beginners. But when used in connection with attempts to straighten out established games those instructions are ineffective because they are concerned with the details rather than the processes and the intents.

Furthermore, they imply a static and sequential readiness of position and posture rather than a dynamic readiness for action. In order to get the same results as the experts the student must supplant sequential execution of details with the carrying out of a correct set of intents with the full cooperation and involvement of the body.

TIMING THE REINFORCEMENT

The coordination of the body action with the swing of the arm is difficult but most critical. Either motion may start too soon or too late relative to the other, the motions may start at the right times but proceed at rates inconsistent with each other, they may be in step with each other but out of synchronization with the ball, or there may be the more usual situation of a combination of several of these problems.

The racquet can be back without the body being back, often to the extent that the body is in the end of stroke position even before the start of the forward swing. Or the player may just allow the body to rotate aimlessly instead of getting it involved in a forward move into the shot. Excessive rotation can also occur, causing a continuous change in racquet direction rather than a consistent heading toward the desired destination.

THE BODY AND ARM AT ODDS

Some players even move the body backwards as they swing and don't realize that they are doing so. The racquet motion is decreased accordingly, and proportionally less energy is stored and recovered. To hit a ball as hard in that case there has to be as much forward movement furnished via arm motion as was subtracted by the backward move of the body.

The loss of velocity involved with energy not stored or not recovered constitutes a severe handicap. At the higher levels of competition, where a player cannot expect to be gifted many cheap points, the amount of energy being expended unnecessarily is often the determining factor as to who loses.

The loud grunts so often heard may merely mean that the arm is being used to its extreme. Not the body, because only a small percentage of the strength of the body is needed to fulfill all of its functions in a stroke. The heavy loading of the arm does not guarantee that the body is also doing its share of the task, and the grunts may even mean that the arm is unnecessarily taking up some of the duties of the body. The sound is not directly produced by the exertion but by holding one's breath and then suddenly releasing it as the effort ends. Thus the noise may be a symbol instead of a result, and therefore may not be really useful or necessary.

DYNAMIC REINFORCEMENT

Reinforcement is an action rather than a static condition. It includes a preparatory turn of the body, cooperation from the body in helping the arm acquire momentum, and timing the sequence so that adequate acceleration is still being maintained when contact with the ball occurs. This should happen at a point where the arm is relatively strong, can still move forward easily, and is backed up by the weight of the body.

By "reinforced" it is meant that the arm is going forward freely on its own and at the same time is being hurried along by the helping but not overpowering force of the shoulder. The impact of the ball is thus met with a more than matching force and is channeled in a rather direct line through the arm into the shoulder, where it is countered by the weight and strength of the body.

However it must be recognized that the workable level of direct reinforcement cannot coincide with the maximum. That maximum would occur at a point where the arm is held straight out in the direction of the ball. The achievable reinforcement during a hit therefore occurs at some point before the maximum, and yet where it can be said that the arm has made a transition from trying to catch up with the shoulder to riding along ahead of it. The proper amount of reinforcement is best developed by just trying to experience it in the feel, not by a conscious positioning of the arm.

If in an emergency a player is caught out of position, the more controlled momentum attained the less direct reinforcement required. Momentum is not a property of the racquet alone. The arm has momentum too, and it is very important because of the great weight of the arm compared with that of the racquet.

OVERDOING IT

Although reinforcement is necessary there ordinarily is too much use of it rather than too little. This is because there is a greater feeling of security obtained by blocking the ball back with reliance on strength than when depending mostly on the momentum of the racquet to do the job. In many critical situations players succumb to a last instant motivation to hit a safe shot with a push rather than a good shot with a swing.

The desire for security causes players to shift the hitting point forward because the ball is easy to see and follow there, and the direct reinforcement is reassuring. This shift is one of the major causes of the deterioration of many player's games when the going gets tough, even for those in the top ranks. The racquet momentum is diminishing out in front instead of increasing, and the reach is becoming limited. In the light of the discussion in the previous chapter about timing complications caused by variations in the hitting point it can be understood how a search for security can result in the opposite.

THE PROBLEMS OF COORDINATION

Satisfying the requirement that the arm not remain behind the body but get at least slightly ahead at impact, and yet have the shoulder moving into the shot at that time, is a very involved accomplishment. The arm has to travel a much greater distance than both the body and the shoulder to come from way behind to slightly ahead.

If the arm is behind and is being pulled rather than pushed forward then the shoulder is getting into the act ahead of its time. If the arm gets too far ahead it begins to be held back by the body and is in danger of being near the limit of its reach. By continually monitoring the feel of the hit the player can learn to avoid the extremes of letting the shoulder stay ahead of the arm or of having the arm lead while the shoulder provides more of a drag than a boost.

When the racquet is being swung forward with maximum available force while the arm is still trying to catch up with the body, then any increase in the rotation of the body at that time will put an unmanageable additional burden on the arm. It then begins to fall behind at an increased rate since there is no unutilized strength left to match the added strain. In that event the reinforcement is either not achieved or is broken if it has been achieved.

There is also no strength left in the arm in that case to counter the impact of the ball, so it is inevitable that the racquet will get jolted backward with respect to the arm. This causes not only further appreciable loss of pace but increased shock to the arm as well. The error rate will rise because when maximum effort is being used the hitting point, timing, attitude of the racquet, and other aspects can be affected in unpredictable ways. The arm should not have to compete with the body, and the body must not begin to exert a forward force on the arm before the arm is allowed to get ahead.

Another eventuality is that the available forward movement of the body, which is not very great distance-wise, will tend to be used up before the time when it is needed most and is most productive: at contact. Enough remaining body motion, through a combination of forward movement and rotation, must be available at contact so as to be able to contribute to the steady acceleration of the racquet. This helps extend the contact interval and improve on the recovery of energies.

It is worth repeating that it is extremely important that the body does not produce significant motion either simultaneously with the arm at the start of its forward motion or too soon thereafter. It is just as important that it not stay behind and do nothing either. Yet even the best people are often not without blame in those respects. Careful observation and analysis will show that even for expert players the strength of the body is often either under or over utilized on all types of strokes. The task for both dubs and pros is to keep the excesses within tolerable limits.

The ideal relationship between the use of the body and the swing of the arm varies with the situation, style, stance, strength, etc., and thus cannot be exactly defined. The criteria to be used are, again, a comfortable feel and the absence of any harmful compensations such as hurrying, roundhouse, freezing the arm, etc. Fortunately, the mastery of the individual elements is achieved by just improving on the intents, satisfactions, and the now enlarged concepts of the hit, rather than by a one by one mastery of the many individual details.

chapter ten

footwork

Footwork is a subordinate item in that it is a means instead of an end. But it is a controlling item in that it occurs first, and in that neither a good swing nor the desired end results are possible if the footwork does not provide for appropriate and timely positioning of the body.

Since the forward motion of the body should be a part of the sequence that combines the final step or adjustment and the actual hit, the getting into position is almost as important as being in position. Being statically ready before the hit is not as good as moving into position at the hit. The final adjustments provided by that last move tend to improve accuracy by optimizing the initial conditions, which together with the momentum generated by the body can result in greatly enhanced power.

A RELUCTANCE TO MOVE

The energy required to move the feet is at least partially recovered in a more effortless and effective swing. However the body does not automatically calculate how to economize on the total use of energy but tends to favor the action that occurs first, and this is where the feet get preferential consideration.

Consequently when a person gets tired the feet may be disinclined to move into proper position. So the body and the arm are then required work harder even though the rewards are likely to be less than normal. There will almost certainly be an increase in the total amount of energy expended.

If the feet are uncooperative, or have a talent for starting out or ending up in unsuitable positions, then difficulties may be created for other elements of a stroke such as the preparation, stance, type of grip, swing, racquet attitude, shoulder turn, involvement of the body, hitting point, aim, and follow-through. Any little deviation in any one of these will normally require extensive compensations elsewhere. Such added complications can go a long way to disorganize one's game.

MIND vs. FEET

As mentioned in the chapter on timing, as the ball approaches closer it appears to move faster and is harder to follow. So to obtain the advantage of having the ball appear to move more slowly than at its actual speed, as well as to improve the view of the other court and satisfy the mindless urge to watch where the ball is intended to go, there is an inclination to hit from a more than usually open stance when one's confidence becomes shaky in critical situations.

Such changes in stance generally cause a rise in errors, and the feet are then often blamed for not wanting to move. But it is an exercise in futility to give directions to the feet to put the body into a stance that is not what the mind and the emotions really want. If the mind and the inner controls can be made to want the proper stance, above the false feelings of security, the feet will obediently make it happen.

There are advantages and disadvantages to each of the different types of stances, so it is not easy to choose one as most suitable even for just a single individual. And of course it is not possible to specify any particular type, as was once thought, as the one right way for everybody. A shot may be good or bad despite the footwork rather than because of it. Although some players with the poorest shots use notably individualistic footwork so too do a few of those with the most strikingly effective shots.

Observation of good players in a tough match may show the feet engaged in a sort of stuttering activity during the wait in the ready position, especially during rapid exchanges at the net. Some of this is not a planned sequence but impulsive reactions to the anticipations of the mind as the player tries to decode the signals that may be evident in the opponent's moves. The footwork usually becomes quite calm again almost as soon as the opponent has made the hit, and the receiver then seems to move with planned ease to the precisely proper spot for the return.

Inexpert players tend to do the opposite, hold a fixed stance too long in the ready position and then, when the ball is well on its way, have to scramble frantically and ineffectively to make the return. In other words, the mind and the body are doing very little during the wait instead of being very actively engaged in anticipation and preparation. The feet of players with too much of a "schooled" technique are possibly waiting to be specifically told to "step out with the near foot" or "cross over with the far foot."

FOOTWORK PATTERNS

There is more emphasis by teachers on the pattern for moving the feet than there probably should be, and probably not enough emphasis on the primary aim of just getting the body ready for the shot. This latter objective lets the feet take care of whatever they have to do to get to wherever have to be for the particular circumstances.

An often cited objective of particular footwork patterns is to try to obtain the furthest reach with the least number of steps. But this does not necessarily equate to the most important consideration: the least amount of time, and to a lesser extent effort, needed to move the necessary distance. The feet usually have adequate training to make the appropriate decisions, or quickly learn.

The number one obligation of the feet is to provide mobility in the shortest time and in the most effective manner in all situations. The mind has the authority to decide that the body has to move somewhere, but it is the prerogative of the feet to decide how to make it happen with neither instruction nor interference. The feet are good at finding ways to fulfill wishes and poor at carrying out specific orders.

While there may be a preferred position of the feet for a particular style of hitting under ideal conditions, the practical rule is to let the feet make the decisions as to the placement needed to help in reinforcing the hit and carrying out the intents for the shot. There may be considerable variation in the footwork for similar strokes as appropriate for such factors as the type of shot received, position in the court, footwork required to get there, momentum of the body, power desired, height of ball, point being aimed at, need for disguise, etc.

Good footwork does not constitute adherence to a prescribed formula and a disregard for the circumstances of the situation, but adaptation to the entire set of details and intentions associated with the shot. There is a tradeoff here in that the adjustments appropriate for specific purposes may come at the cost of providing tip-offs to the opponent if the footwork has an observable relationship to the outcome.

Of course clumsy movements should be noted and gradually eliminated, but otherwise the automatic responses of the feet ought not be subject to fixed rules and conscious attention, especially during the exigencies of actual play. Intellectualizing the activities of the feet at times when it is necessary that they use their own good judgement and ability to react and improvise is hardly progress. The feet learn a lot from everyday experience, and a tennis game is not the occasion to let that education go to waste in favor of predetermined patterns, oversimplified assumptions, and time consuming decisions.

What the feet can do when called on very suddenly depends quite a bit on what they happen to be doing at the moment. Just about anybody's feet can find a number of good ways to do whatever is called for, but it is not evident that minds have the ability to devise similarly varied and appropriate solutions for the feet on the spur of the moment. Patterns can be more useful as illustrations of choices than as prescribed reactions under set conditions. They may be useful in some normal situations, but can be a handicap when the unusual occurs.

THE FOOTWORK FOR SPECIAL SITUATIONS

Compensations are required in other elements of the stroke when the responses of the feet are not suitable for a particular situation. This sets off a related chain of adjustments to restore compatibility, and if they are not made serious errors in execution may ensue, especially in the timing of individual elements. One probable result that happens to be easy to both overlook and underestimate is loss of naturalness.

When a ball is taken at some other height than is most convenient there is a tendency not to move the feet. The basic reason for the neglect is that the player doesn't know how to hit the ball at the inconvenient height, so the feet aren't told where the body wants to go and don't get trained in where to move and how to get set properly. They cooperate as dutifully with indecision and wrong decision as with sound intents.

Lack of effective footwork when the ball cannot be taken at a preferred height is most unfortunate because in such situations getting into position, using as decent a swing as possible, and meeting the ball within the available hitting zone have even more than their normal importance. It is therefore wise to get a lot of practice in hitting off of uncomfortable bounces. An added reason is that the hitting zone tends to narrow as the height of the hitting point departs from what is most convenient. A match is not the place to start solving the problems with such difficulties.

Of course the first choice with uncomfortable bounces would always be to drift forward or back to be able to use a customary swing at a convenient height. Inexpert players tend to stand in the vicinity of the baseline and take the ball at whatever height it happens to have when it gets there. As a rule they are not too willing to move up from the baseline and have an even greater reluctance to move back. There is no overall saving of energy here, and the penalty in terms of results can be very consequential.

JUMPING DURING THE HIT

Even after getting properly into position many people will decrease the effectiveness of the shot by jumping and turning to face the net during the hit, perhaps even before. Some of this is due to the intent to watch where the ball is going, or the desire to get ready for the next shot. For many people it is instigated by a desire to batter every ball for an untouchable winner.

But jumping with that purpose involves a misconception as to how to use the body to obtain maximum power. It is doubtful that any extra pace can be obtained by lifting both feet off the ground since there is some loss of forward shift of the body, and of bracing between arm, body, and the ground. The jump is often conducive to roundhouse, which is not a good means of developing pace. The body is more than strong enough to turn or move into the hit on its own without the extra flourish of a jump.

It is not wrong per se to jump, or to turn while doing so. The actions do facilitate viewing the ball and the other side of the court, getting ready for the next shot, and getting a quick start for an advance to the net. A major problem is that the jump is often a rather uncontrolled and emotional action that is conducive of error. Just as the force of the swing can vary with emotions and intents, so can the jump. This added source of variation will sometimes have unfortunate consequences on the execution and direction of the hit. Once the jump starts there is little possibility of any last instant adjustment of the position of the body to compensate for any sudden quirky behavior of the oncoming ball.

THE CENTER LINE THEORY

A very common but oversimplified bit of advice is to always return as quickly as possible to the central area behind the baseline after every shot. This involves a sizable effort if the player has been drawn wide to either side. Furthermore, when a player is arriving at that central point the momentum is still pulling heavily to keep the body going in the same direction at the same speed, particularly after a desperate run. To reverse course completely at that time and run back the full half-width of the court presents a real problem. The opponent can easily take advantage of that difficulty by hitting back to the same side.

There is another often taught strategy that works better in such situations. If a player merely heads for the central area, but slows down so as not to get all the way back before the opponent hits the ball, it is still just as easy or even easier to cover the far side of the court because of already being in motion in that direction. When in motion it is possible to cover a much greater distance in the same direction than when a start has to be made from a dead stop, or when a reversal of direction is required.

The further a receiver has been drawn wide on a shot the faster will the return journey to the central area have to be, and the more distance can be covered while continuing in the same direction. If the opponent hits back to the same side this may also not present a particular problem because, although a stop and reversal of direction are required, the receiver will not yet have reached the center line and will be less than half the width of the court from the sideline from which the retreat was being made.

ADVANCING TO THE NET

A similar line of reasoning applied in the case of advancing toward the net is not as valid because it is not advisable to be caught in no-man's-land. A ball hit low into this area by the opponent is difficult to handle, especially if hit hard. So when advancing to the net it is necessary to get up to approximate volleying position as quickly as possible.

But instead of coming to a dead stop with the feet in a straddle position a little remaining forward momentum is very useful because it can be easily redirected toward either side, and in a shorter time and with faster court coverage and less effort than when having to start with no initial momentum at all. Although coming to a stop with the feet spread gives great balance it is not conducive to easy sideways movement. A wide spread decreases the available length of the push and presents too much inertia located too far out to allow for a quick start in either sideward direction.

THE OPEN STANCE

The following discussion of the open stance refers basically to the forehand since on the backhand a sideways stance is almost mandatory. A player does not have to choose between just open or closed, however, since any degree of in-between can be used. In this book the terms "open stance" and "facing the net" refer mainly to those shots that are made with the chest largely parallel to the net, regardless of how the feet are planted.

A serious problem with hitting while facing the net is that the arm is not free to go very far in either the backward or forward directions. Hence both the backswing and follow-through are not as long as they could be as when facing sideways. Therefor the timing with the shortened swing has to be exceptionally accurate in order to have the racquet meet the ball at the best point within the narrow available hitting zone.

Since the use of the open stance involves a compression of the time and space available to develop the required racquet momentum there may be sudden and large demands on the arm and shoulder muscles. The open stance is therefore somewhat unsuitable for most women. They generally tend to favor a more closed stance, or at least a decided preparatory turn of the torso. Either of these options allows use of a relatively long swing to develop the necessary racquet momentum without putting potentially damaging strain on the arm and shoulder.

If an open stance results in a loss of ball velocity the opponent will be given added time to make the return. That person may then dominate the exchange sufficiently to have the other player scurrying back and forth just barely able to make retrievals. The initial advantage of an economy of effort in getting into position then becomes quite the opposite in chasing down the returns. Added disadvantages with the open stance are that it is not conducive to good reinforcement of the shot with the body, and does not permit easy enhancement of the pace by moving the body into the hit.

On the other hand, if the hips and torso are initially rotated well backward during the preparation they can then be reversed and rotated forward during the forward swing to develop very satisfactory results. In other words the body gets wound up something like a spring, and body strength and movement augment those of the arm for a possibly impressive increase in power.

The timing in this case is again very critical. If the rotation of the body is early it will leave the arm behind and cause an ineffective hit, and will be conducive to racquet motion around the body instead of forward in the direction of the ball. If the rotation is late the stroke will probably deteriorate into an arm alone swing and will fail to generate the desired racquet momentum.

Positive aspects of the open stance include minimizing the time and effort required to get into position, and allowing easy movement or change of movement toward either side. The open stance stroke is relatively short, economizing on the time required to finish, and so further eases the problems of getting ready for the next shot. It allows unrestricted view of the ball and the other side of the court. It permits easy camouflage of the direction of the hit. It is compatible with the Western forehand grip, which is widely used to deal with high bounces and to get heavy topspin. When the player gets tired there tends to be less degeneration in the positioning of the feet and the body than with a sideways stance.

THE CLOSED STANCE

The closed stance maximizes the available length of the swing. This makes it easy to develop racquet momentum, accelerate through contact, vary the hitting point within a deep hitting zone, have freedom of arm in the follow-through, and hit down the line or cross court to either side. It provides good arm strength yet also reduces the need for a large amount of strength in the arm. It moderates damage to the arm, provides good reinforcement of the arm with the body at the hit, and allows the body and the shoulder to be moved or rotated into the hit. It works especially well with the Eastern grip and variations.

On the negative side, the view of the other court is somewhat restricted with the sideways stance. Added effort by the feet is required to get the body into position. For that reason a tired player has more of a tendency to neglect getting into position with the closed stance than with the open. Getting back into the face-the-net position between strokes takes added effort, and if that move is late it may throw off the timing of the next stroke. While the timing of the hit is simplified because of the deep hitting zone, it is at the same time made somewhat difficult because the strokes are long, requiring that the timing be started earlier and be continued over a greater interval than for a short stroke.

A MODIFIED CLOSED STANCE

On the forehand the "net" foot (closest to the net) need not be the foot that is forward (closest to the path of the ball). The "fence" foot (farthest from the net) can be the one placed forward even though the stance remains partially or even totally sideways in terms of the attitude of the chest. The positioning of the feet is open in this case, but the direction in which they point and the attitude of the body can be partially or totally sideways.

This stance can be approximated from the ready position by just partly turning the body and the feet toward the side and repositioning the feet slightly. The hit is made from a truly sideways position, and is not the same as that other previously described similar shot hit from a more completely open stance. The upper part of the body can be rotated backward to assume a closed attitude, and can be put in a strong tension for release into the forward swing.

In this in-between posture the balance is naturally and suitably forward into the hit. It is apt to be used quite frequently on the forehand just because of the minimum time and effort needed to shift between the ready and hitting positions. As in the open stance, the body is not in the way of the arm as the racquet goes into the follow-through. However the above advantages are not being cited as a recommendation of the stance over the other options.

Notes on

watching the ball · · · ·

chapter eleven
watching the ball - - - -

It has been said that a person's knowledge of any subject diminishes and disappears at the rate of ninety percent per year as soon as the study of it is discontinued. So a person is either advancing in an intellectual sense or declining at a precipitous rate. There is no such thing as staying on an intellectual plateau if a good level and amount of intellectual activity is not maintained. It takes hard running just to stay in place.

Somewhat the same may be true of tennis skills, but here the decline can set in even without any drop in activity. One reason is that as the game gets better the rate of improvement necessarily declines, so it is eventually exceeded by the rate of deterioration. Another reason is that once a high level of play is achieved there is a false expectation that the level can be maintained in spite of a continual drop in the aims and in both the physical and mental efforts.

The remedy being proposed for this situation is to base execution as much on satisfactions and the goal of continual improvement as on winning points. Trying to upgrade the satisfactions promotes the expenditure of the required level of effort, and creates aversion and awareness of the return of old flaws or the intrusion of any new. The means to accomplish these objectives rests largely on the previously explained self-monitoring processes and a knowledge of the principles of hitting.

Some of the major avenues to deterioration are failing to form a proper set of intentions for the hit, economizing on the preparation, succumbing to emotional urges and impulses, seeking impossible results through the use of unworkable techniques, failing to recognize both the satisfactions and the unpleasantnesses of each experience, and allocating attention to details instead of main ideas.

CONCENTRATING ON DETAILS

When a person's game begins to fall apart the usual remedy of increasing the attention paid to some single element or function, such as the ball, stance, hitting point, or follow-through, is not really useful or wise, especially if it is not known for sure whether or not the requirements for that element are already being sufficiently taken care of, or that there is any connection to the problems being experienced.

In most circumstances such preoccupation amounts to upsetting the balance of attention being paid to the many things that are happening largely automatically. For that reason allocating special attention to individual elements may induce deterioration rather than improvement in the overall execution. This may help explain why in many cases the harder one tries the worse things get. Nevertheless the player must not be completely unaware of details either, even though they should not be the subject of specific observation.

Conscious attention and decision are probably best reserved for strategy, analysis, visualization of the hit, the timing of the development of racquet momentum if necessary, evaluation of the last shot, etc. It should not be wasted on a major or minor detail of execution, especially since in tennis there may only be time to do it and not think about it. If there is deliberate mental control of any element of the stroke, such as racquet attitude, movement of the feet, or tightening of the grip, it may be possible to obtain improvement by merely letting the body make the necessary provisions on its own.

It is as unrealistic to believe that watching the ball will automatically cure whatever internal or external timing difficulty is being experienced as it is to believe that timing involves nothing more than having the racquet meet the ball at a proper hitting point. It is only necessary to reflect back on the complexity of the timing processes, as discussed in the chapter on that subject, to become convinced that it takes much more than watching the ball to obtain a solution for the various possible types of difficulties with timing.

An unfortunate effect of trying to watch the ball is that the eye may gradually begin to concentrate on the departure instead of the approach, a natural development in itself. So in that case the process eventually ends up being self-defeating by focusing attention on the wrong event. Preoccupation with where the ball is going is assigning priority to what can no longer be helped, and at the cost of detracting attention from where it can do the most good: the hit.

PRIMARY *vs.* SUBSIDIARY

The detail of watching the ball is subsidiary to that of timing in the same way that the detail of timing is subsidiary to the concepts of the swing and the hit. Watching the ball is thus at least three levels removed from the primary concern, the hit. Therefor paying special attention to the lower level detail does not guarantee that the higher level items to which it is subsidiary will be correspondingly improved thereby.

If a player is getting near optimum racquet momentum and acceleration at impact, a minimum of last instant compensations, a feel of the ball landing on the "sweet spot" of the racquet, and of the arm being properly reinforced with the body at impact, all with some ease and consistency from shot to shot, then the ball is being watched neither too little nor too much. And, as the saying goes, "if it isn't wrong don't fix it."

Most people do not really neglect to observe the ball enough. They rather do not pay enough attention to the hit as a whole, usually in favor of concentrating on the intended destination of the ball instead. To "keep your eye on the ball" is neither a directly useful process nor an end in itself.

This kind of watching is particularly harmful since it is taking place during the entire swing interval. It is a subordinate activity, and is important only to the extent that it can affect the quality of other details on the same or other levels that are themselves directly useful. These latter can therefore be called the "functional" factors because they perform useful functions.

EVALUATION OF QUALITY

It is not wrong to observe the ball to some extent, since whatever is sufficient in that way will actually also be indispensable to the achievement of a good hit. A better way is to just "be aware" without doing any conscious watching. A person can be aware of many details but can watch only one, or at best several.

While the intent to "watch the ball" may be proper the instruction may even be considered to be technically unsound and possibly harmful. The effect is to diminish the awareness of other items that fulfill the additional function of providing some qualitative evaluation of the functional elements. Nevertheless it has come to be considered somewhat of a cure-all.

The overall feel of the quality of the stroke, from preparation through contact, is a matter that gets very little attention but that should be of major concern on every shot. Continual sensing of this attribute tends to optimize the factors producing the satisfying feel that is one of the most reliable measures of a good hit.

The process of evaluating the quality of a shot focuses attention for brief moments in nonspecific ways on the details that count as they occur, and may also automatically create an awareness of compromises and deficiencies as they intrude into the functional elements. There is brief peripheral attention to many details instead of conscious concentration on just a few, or only one.

OBSERVING INTERNAL ITEMS

When a person's strokes are not working, and evaluation of the quality of the hit does not seem to provide any leads as to the source of the problems, then it may be time to investigate the more specific details of execution. But instead of watching the ball, which is an external item, it may be better to examine observable circumstances of the internal events and actions involved in the stroke.

An ideal form of that something might be described as a circumstance that provides some sort of appraisal of the level of excellence of the stroke as a whole. It should involve a precise critical moment and should be transitory so that it cannot be watched before or after that moment. Even this type of directed observation should generally be used only as a temporary expedient. Specific details are normally not worthy of individual attention, and all the other details do not deserve to be correspondingly neglected.

Some suggestions for items that might be suitable for such observation are: the degree of readiness just before the swing starts forward, the appropriateness of the body position with respect to the hitting point, the position of impact lengthwise along the face of the racquet or in the way of being off center toward an edge, etc.

All of these items involve a fleeting awareness of several characteristics of the stroke, not just the approach of the ball. But observing the ball is automatically included to some extent. There is no attempt to change a technique or force a result but to obtain an awareness of a circumstance. Instead of the strokes being just automatic reflexes, unmonitored and unevaluated, a little awareness of the mechanics and the quality of the shot is obtained.

Other types of observations involve actions or activities. Examples of these are the participation of the body, smoothness or compulsiveness of the swing, direction of the swing going forward or roundhouse, condition of the arm in the way of being cramped inward or extended comfortably outward, adequacy of the momentum of the racquet, nature of the follow-through, use of push, presence of compensations, the arm getting and staying ahead of the body or being dragged along behind, the arm moving freely at impact or nearing the end of its reach, etc.

The items in the last paragraph are actions instead of circumstances. Here there is always a danger of a loss of naturalness or even workability if an action that occurs automatically becomes the object of conscious monitoring or mental direction. On the other hand, if it just so happens that the detail is associated with a known or unknown deficiency the reward for closer examination may be a refinement of the strokes even when things are already working quite well.

It is not being suggested in the above discussion to try to see the ball meet the strings since that, if possible at all, is beyond the capabilities of most players. It is also not particularly useful. Nevertheless that skill may be within the means of a few people with exceptional eyesight, and for them it might be a useable option. The occasionally heard advice to "follow the ball into the racquet with the eyes" is also not being suggested. It is not that easy to define when to commence and when to end following the ball, and there doesn't seem to be much possibility of obtaining an evaluation of the quality of a function in that manner.

It is possible that no solutions can be found by means of the observation of either circumstances or actions, and that there may even be a consequent worsening of the problems, especially if the process degenerates into detailed examination instead of general awareness. But occasionally an investigation may turn up something of value, and in the meantime the continual use and refinement of the techniques of observation and evaluation will have a growth of efficiency and effectiveness in themselves.

AWARENESS OF STANDARDS

Another beneficial fallout from such self observation is that it may help to define and perfect the personal requirements for specific techniques. These standards may have use as sort of benchmarks when problems develop and one's game begins to falter. It may be useful to discover the events or actions that are related to either a consistent personal problem or an exceptional success. It is unwise to wait to investigate such relationships until when the answers are urgently needed in a match, or have resort at that time only to "watch the ball."

The proper degree of emphasis is best assured by subordinating the detail to the accomplishment of the major task. If a player has the right natural instincts it may not be necessary to be concerned with the details of execution. It may even be a mistake to do so. But when wrong intentions, urges, understandings, etc., creep in it is necessary to have some idea of what is normal so that the wrong tendencies can be quickly identified and eliminated.

It is extremely difficult to specify exactly what should be happening at impact. For that reason no definition is being attempted for the exact attitude of the racquet at any time, or the point of impact, or any other standard for whatever particular item one chooses to observe. If the feel is good, and the sense of what is good is being continually refined, that is what counts regardless of the possible presence of supposedly inappropriate elements. It may be useful to know what is happening but it is dangerous to assume that it is firmly known what amounts to perfection and should be happening.

The above discussions were partly designed to prevent overemphasis on what is one of the most sacred dogmas of tennis instruction. Attention must be paid to the ball to try to accurately judge its speed, distance, direction, spin, and bounce. Even expert players tend to become more interested in watching the other side of the court than in paying the required amount of attention to what is happening on their own.

Many inexpert players are so careless in that respect that errant hits are a frequent consequence. For them it may in fact be desirable to put extra emphasis on "watch the ball." But perhaps even there it may be better to watch one of the other mentioned circumstances or actions to realize the additional advantages obtained from qualitative evaluation.

The people who are most likely to go to unnecessary extremes in trying to watch the ball are those who do not learn easily from experience, or do not have good athletic ability, and therefore may take instruction so literally as to defeat the objectives of what in moderation could be perfectly good advice.

REACTIONS IN DIFFICULT SITUATIONS

A particular situation where there usually is insufficient attention paid to both the internal and external details of a stroke is in the case when it is barely possible to get to the ball and make any kind of return at all. The three most common errors of execution are: (1) not to make timely preparation and yet (2) reach out and hit too far out in front because (3) the fear of being late causes excessive hurrying of the swing.

Merely "watching the ball" does not make any direct provision to address any of these three items. In fact watching any specific technique or operation in this case is conducive to neglect of not only the above problems but the major factor that is conspicuously missing: formulating the intentions for the normal or special preparations required for the hit. This preliminary must always be accomplished, although only in a subconscious manner, to have a chance that the mechanics of the hit will be working for the success of the shot, especially in those situations where getting back any kind of return at all is an achievement.

AWARENESS OF NEGATIVES AND POSITIVES

Ordinarily the best consul about paying attention to details is to just be aware of the quality of execution and to notice a detail in particular only when something unusual occurs, terrible or terrific. Among the negative features that can be noticed in that way are body not readied, late start of swing, wrong hitting point, arm cramped inward, unpleasant feel, body movement not used or not coordinated with the arm, forward swing hurried, push instead of swing, racquet head not up to required momentum, slapping instead of hitting, use of roundhouse, etc.

Harmless mannerisms can be ignored, but there must be awareness of any compensations being used as this may be a tip-off that a technique is present that does not readily fit into the pattern of the swing. It is wise to pay attention to the positive side also, appreciating the items that were good in the stroke just as much as bemoaning what was bad. Anything especially good or especially bad should trigger a slight suggestion in the mind as to the nature of the goodness or the badness. Know and feel when something is exceptional in how you prepare, move, stand, swing, make contact, end up, etc. Do not "watch the ball," "bend the knees," and "follow-through" but intend to achieve a quality hit.

There is an old theory about the classic ground strokes that the face of the racquet should remain perfectly perpendicular to the ground during at least the latter part of the forward swing, and especially during contact. The idea probably grew out of the teaching of the elementary techniques to novices, with the student hitting straight out off waist high bounces set up for the purpose by the instructor. However the theory is not consistent with such other commonly heard advice as "hit up on the ball," "roll the racquet over the ball," and "the ball should clear the net by at least two feet."

OLD THEORIES SELDOM FADE AWAY

There are at least three reasons why the idea of keeping the racquet face perpendicular to the ground should probably have been abandoned long ago: (1) Details do not deserve conscious attention but should be executed automatically. (2) No justifications or benefits have been cited or proved. (3) It is not true that the racquet face must necessarily be perpendicular during any part of the swing in any style of stroke.

It should again be pointed out that talented players learn and do whatever works particularly well without necessarily being consciously aware of exactly what that is or how it is accomplished. But it seems that when these people become instructors they recite the rigid rules that had been taught to them when they were novices. They generally neglect recommending or explaining the modifications that they themselves had subsequently adopted.

FACTORS AFFECTING THE RACQUET ATTITUDE

The fact that the face of the racquet is generally not at right angles with the ground, even at the actual hit, can be very easily proved. If a player's shots are landing short the usual correction that will automatically occur will be a slight upward adjustment of the racquet attitude to raise the trajectory of the ball. And if the ball is carrying too far the racquet attitude will be automatically adjusted in the other direction, all mostly under the intent to change the trajectory and destination of the ball rather than specifically to adjust the racquet angle. So even if the face would be perpendicular in one case it would not be so in the other.

If anybody is thinking that the up or down adjustment needed to achieve the correct racquet attitude would be the one that would place the face of the racquet in a vertical position then consider the following. If the pace is to be changed on similar hits but the target area is intended to remain the same, the attitude of the racquet must be altered to lift the trajectory higher or bring it lower, as the case may be, to compensate for the changed carrying power of the ball. Conversely, if the pace is to remain the same but the depth is to be changed then some adjustment in the attitude of the racquet is again required to do the job.

Of course some people expect to have the ball land short or deep as desired without making any associated changes. An example is a person trying to vary the depths of the shots while never changing the intent to hit as hard as possible or have the ball do other than just barely clear the net. In that event if the intent to hit deep succeeds in getting the ball to just clear the net the usual outcome of the intent to hit short is a ball that lands in the net. Some adjustment has to be made someplace.

Carrying the racquet upward as well as forward is an alternative means of lifting the trajectory of the ball. However if the upward move is strong enough to create a great deal of topspin the ball may drop so fast that it has to be directed up in a high loop to compensate. The attitude of the racquet may then again have to be tilted a little more upward for that task than for a flat shot.

The nature of the bounce off the type of surface being used has an effect on how the racquet has to be faced. Taking a ball that is rising at some specific rate and angle requires a different racquet attitude than when taking a ball that is rising more slowly, or at a different angle, or is not rising at all, or is actually on the way down.

Underspin shots are almost always hit with an open racquet face (tilted up). Other reasons for adjustment include variation in the height at which the ball is hit, the position in the court, the choice of straight or looping trajectories, the compensations required for wind conditions, and the amount and type of spin received or returned. Variations in the stance also create problems with the verticality concept since the stance affects the nature of the swing, the racquet attitude, and the pace and spin of the ball.

HITTING STRAIGHT OUT

If the bottom of a ball is exactly three feet off the ground when the ball is hit straight out with a perpendicular racquet face there is no way that the ball can clear the net since the lowest point of the net is also at three feet. Any slight drop due to gravity will bring the ball down below net level before the net is reached.

So even at this approximately ideal hitting height the ball has to be directed upward by one means or another. Consequently most ground strokes that are not hit with at least some upward move of the racquet, and are also not hit while the ball is on the rise, require that the racquet face be tilted slightly upward to compensate for the effects of gravity.

EXTRA MANIPULATIONS

Any player who has learned to hit with consistency has learned to employ whatever racquet angle is required for the particular style being used. There is nevertheless the possibility that even an expert player's strokes will contain unnecessary flourishes in the attitude of the racquet, a few that are of no consequence but most being at least slightly detrimental.

Some of these extra flourishes may really be the finish of compensations that began while the ball was still in contact with the racquet. Others may just be due to a futile effort to influence the ball after contact has ended. If any seemingly unnecessary alteration of the attitude of the racquet does not interfere with the hit, and is also not a compensation for another problem, then there is no great reason to be concerned even if the motion has no discernible useful purpose.

But during impact there should be little in the way of sudden changes of attitude except as required by the particular technique, or for special effects, or as a means of adjustment for unanticipated problems. If sudden changes are constantly being used then that could be due to recognition by the body and the subconscious mind of the need to make compensations for flaws in the technique. As an example, a perpendicular racquet attitude during the swing may make it necessary to turn the wrist upward rather quickly at the hit.

A gradual variation in the racquet attitude may be a functional part of some styles of hitting, as for instance in the case of the rolling of the racquet associated with the Western forehand grip. Depending on the grip and style used, the racquet may start forward very open or very closed or anywhere in between, and there may be a continuous change in attitude through most of the stroke, including during contact.

TIMING THE CHANGE

A change in racquet attitude requires a timing of that change, and that entails coordination with the timing of everything else. If any other element is mistimed then an adjustment may be required to the normal timing of the changes in the attitude. For an illustration: if the hitting point occurs elsewhere than at the usual place then the location where any particular slant of the racquet would normally occur must be shifted forward or backward accordingly so as to have the racquet end up with the correct attitude at impact.

A large part of the very complicated timing process has to shift along with the hitting point. By a parallel line of reasoning, it is very difficult to change the timing of any single element because the subconscious mind and the muscles will resist making changes to the customary timing of the many associated elements.

REASON INSTEAD OF RULES

The cited problems with the advice to keep the racquet face perpendicular provide additional arguments for not imposing conscious control over details, but rather letting the body do whatever seems to be necessary. It is obvious that a player who takes the perpendicularity rule as faith, and who is apt to make a special attempt to observe that restriction when unidentified problems occur, is merely heading for bigger troubles. This is especially true if a simultaneous effort is made to follow other rules of similar validity. As the saying goes: "a little knowledge is a dangerous thing." And particularly if it is wrong.

WHEN THE BALL TILTS THE RACQUET

Sometimes the tilting of the racquet is accidental, as when a hit that is off center toward either edge of the racquet causes a momentary change in the racquet attitude. The consequence will often be a pronounced and unwanted effect on the rebound angle of the ball. The change in racquet attitude caused by an off center hit happens so quickly as to be quite imperceptible to most players. But it is there and nobody is strong enough to stop it completely.

The degree of the tilt depends on such things as the momentum of the racquet and of the ball, the size and characteristics of the racquet, the distance of the hit off center, and the strength of the player's grip. The tilt and the effect on the rebound will be upward if the location of the hit is off center toward the top edge of the racquet, and downward if the location is toward the bottom edge.

If off center hits are the usual circumstance the player is likely to become accustomed to the feel and will probably come to consider it as normal, and thus may have little inkling as to the cause of the equally usual erratic behavior of the ball. The reader by this time would not be likely to entertain the idea that a permanent cure could be obtained by such means as watching the ball, keeping the racquet face perpendicular, or even by just squeezing the grip at impact.

COMPLEXITIES OF THE REBOUND ANGLE

When a ball approaches the center of the racquet at some angle to the face of the racquet, as is usually true to some extent, it will bounce off at an angle that is opposite in direction but approximately the same in magnitude, the way light does off a mirror. The word "approximately" is used because a ball has weight and therefore does not behave in exactly the same way as light. And the rule is reasonably valid only if the ball has no spin and the receiver's racquet is either held strictly stationary or is moving the other way along the same path as the approaching ball. When those conditions are satisfied the rule is essentially true regardless of the speed of the ball relative to the racquet.

The result is different if the racquet is moving at some angle to the path of the ball because the "apparent" impact angle is then not the same as the real. The "apparent" angle, which is what the player sees, is just an instantaneous snapshot of the path of the ball with respect to the face of the racquet. Suffice it to say here that the true angle depends on the vector combination of the speeds and directions of both the racquet and the ball. The eye has no way of making such calculations and therefore the player has no way of seeing the real angle.

The faster the racquet travels the more importance does the racquet have in determining both the "effective" speed of the ball and the real impact angle. What this means to the player is that the faster the racquet moves the more does it control the direction of the rebound. The ability to correctly anticipate such effects on the rebound angle is part of what is called "racquet feel." Many people do not have much of it, so this analysis is being provided to help develop that quality where it is missing.

If when a player gets nervous or emotional the hit is made with either the extreme of too much caution or that of too much desire there are apt to be variations from the norm in racquet velocity. The real impact angle of the ball and the angle of rebound may then be affected in unexpected ways because of the relationships mentioned above. So here is another situation where there can be unanticipated effects arising out of physical principles with which many players are not familiar, either intuitively or actually.

SPIN AND THE REBOUND ANGLE

Still another variable influence on the rebound angle is that the strings bite in and hold on very firmly when a ball is hit hard, and thus overcome the spin forces that try to send the ball off at an angle. Those forces do not disappear but become comparatively less significant on hard hits, and also become dissipated by internal friction.

If an oncoming ball that has considerable spin is met softly most of the energy of the spin is not stored but is expended in rolling the ball across the face of the racquet. When the ball is hit much harder the rolling action is prevented by the flattening of the ball. The energy of the spin then gets to be stored as a deformation of a side of the cover. But when that deformation snaps back it tends to send the ball off in a direction opposite to what the ball would have taken had it just rolled across the strings.

If the ball is hit very hard the rolling action is suppressed almost completely, and the sideways deformation and the angular force created by the spin become proportionately less important compared with the force and direction of the racquet. There can then also be a relatively inelastic crushing of the ball, in which case the forces due to spin become both comparatively small and also get lost in the unproductive crushing action. The effects of spin on the rebound angle can then become rather inconsequential.

COMBINATIONS OF THE FORCES OF SPIN

When only a part of the energy of the spin is stored then the part that is not stored tries to roll the ball across the face of the racquet in one direction while the stored energy tries to send the ball off in the opposite direction. The combination of the opposing forces exerted by the stored and unstored rotational energies at various impact velocities can cause the ball to leave in unexpected directions. As a result the direction of departure of the ball is often a matter of surprise even though always strictly a matter of cause and effect.

Note the complexity of the demands on the reflexes, with the correct attitude of the racquet being dependant on the relative dominance of the direction, momentum, and firmness of the racquet over the momentum, direction, and spin of the ball. The correct adjustment has to be a matter of experience, instinct, intention, and art rather than simple rules and conscious calculation.

The actual or intuitive knowledge of the controlling principles can prevent misconceptions as well as too easy acceptance of all-inclusive rules, and can reduce the number of errors or at least the false assignment of blame for errant hits. The majority of talented players hit properly without being specifically aware of these principles, but the rules cannot just be ignored because they are what the ball always obeys.

chapter thirteen

the backswing

In order to evaluate the choices available on the back-swing it is necessary to supply brief descriptions of some of the techniques. These are intended as gener-alized outlines for the purpose of discussion of the problems and the advantages, and not as directions for the specific means of execution, or as recommenda-tions for a particular style.

THE STRAIGHT BACKSWING

The classic method of taking the racquet back from a face-the-net waiting position starts with a one quarter turn of the upper body, carrying the racquet arm along also. The quarter turn places the upper torso in a side-ways stance with the racquet pointing toward the side of the court, already about half way to the end of the backswing.

Next the hips and the feet are swiveled around in a continuation of the turn, and a step is made across the body with the far foot (the one furthest from the path of the ball). At the same time the racquet continues the rest of the way to the end of the backswing carried by the existing momentum and the use of a little additional exertion by the arm and shoulder.

While the technique as described is too rigid and methodical for most shots in actual play it is a fairly good way to start learning the essentials of the backswing, and it has the advantage of deterring the development of wild and unnecessary manipulations of the racquet. A few tournament players use the general form of the method on ground strokes, but there are many others who use techniques that if not better are at least more fluid.

NO EXERTION BY THE ARM?

However a little examination and analysis reveals that the claims for the advantages of the classic backswing are not as technically sound as may at first seem. Even if the arm is just carried along, and is not moved independently during the initial quarter turn of the body, the arm has to exert effort in overcoming the restraining pull created by the inertia of the racquet.

The force needed to overcome that inertia is dependant on four things: (1) the total mass of the racquet, (2) the location of its center of gravity, (3) the distance at which the racquet is held out from the body, and (4) the rate at which the racquet is accelerated. It is obvious that the force is independent of the source of the motion, whether due to the turn of the body or the swing of the arm.

Holding the arm fixedly out in front so that the racquet is carried around by the initial rotation of the body, as in the start of the simplified classic backswing, encounters just as much resistance to acceleration and requires just as much exertion by the arm as when the body is held still and the racquet is taken back with the arm alone.

Rather than that the muscles of the arm and shoulder are relieved of any effort, they must overcome the inertia of the arm and the racquet so that both will be accelerated sufficiently to keep up with the rotation of the body. In the process the arm muscles may occasionally even be strained beyond their limits since the body is very strong, and may turn more quickly than the arm muscles can conveniently force the arm and racquet to follow.

STOP AND RESTART

As the racquet approaches the end of this classic "straight" backswing the motion must be stopped and then restarted in the opposite direction. The restart must be made early enough so that the reversal is not too sudden or tiring, and does not cause a strain that gets to be damaging. If the backswing is late the reversal of motion has to be hurried, and the buildup of the forward racquet momentum will probably not progress quite as well, or at least not as easily, as without the handicap of the lateness.

A consequence of trying to make up for a tardy backswing is that the impact of the ball occurs during the unpropitious interval when the arm is subject to the strain involved in hurriedly overcoming the combined inertia of itself and the racquet. This will produce the unpleasant and damaging jolt that is the customary experience of armies of players, not always entirely restricted to those of the lower echelons.

THE LOOP BACKSWING

A widely used alternative to the classic "straight" method is the "loop" backswing. In this process, instead of being taken straight back, the racquet head is rotated to the end position, usually at a level that is higher than that at which it will be brought forward. When the racquet head has looped all the way back in the upper path and begins the move downward into the forward path, the need for extra effort for the gradual increase in speed that is required at that time is minimized by an assist from the force of gravity.

Effort is further reduced in that racquet momentum is being continuously redirected via the loop rather than stopped and restarted, and in that moving the racquet back while held close in reduces the inertia of the racquet and the consequent burden on the arm compared with when the racquet is held out and away.

The conservation of momentum, the cooperation of gravity, and the easing of the burden on the arm can be very helpful in maintaining pace and consistency when tiredness sets in, or in making it possible to get a good measure of extra pace when desired. The same factors tend to prevent the onset of tennis elbow, or help to minimize the damage of continued play if the elbow is already hurting.

The motion of the loop backswing is very fluid. While this is very desirable in itself it has the disadvantage of making it easy to exaggerate the motion. The racquet head should follow a rather compact ellipse conveniently close in, not huge circles, and not either as close to the body or as far from it as possible. But here again some players manage to exaggerate with singular success. Billy Johnson of the Bill Tilden era, and with reputedly one of the greatest forehands of all time, is said to have used a loop backswing that often took the racquet back at about the full extension of his arm above his head.

Although the racquet goes back in a curve with the use of the loop technique the forward swing should ordinarily be fairly straight, even when the racquet is made to follow an upwardly angled path for the purpose of topspin. While continuation of the circular motion into the forward swing is not necessarily wrong, it can complicate timing, interfere with an adequate follow-through, require extra arm effort to accelerate against gravity, and take away from the forward velocity of racquet and ball.

ELBOW FIRST TECHNIQUE

With either of the two described backswings there are two partially simultaneous actions involved in getting the racquet back: (1) moving the whole arm back and (2) unfolding or extending the lower arm to place the racquet head in its final ready position poised for the forward swing. Some players separate these actions on the forehand by using an elbow first technique, really just a variation of the loop method. This backswing involves "leading with the elbow," which for many years was considered to be a taboo.

Instead of the body being rotated to "carry" the arm and the racquet back as in the "straight" backswing, or of the racquet being moved through a vertical arc as in the loop, in this third method the racquet and lower arm are pulled along behind the elbow. As the initial pulling motion decreases the arm unfolds backward, and the racquet head continues in a loop to the end position. The backward loop of the racquet head is often, although not preferably, slightly downward. If this becomes pronounced it creates an inefficiency because the downward motion does not flow as easily into the forward swing as does an initial upward loop.

Taking the racquet back in this way, comfortably close in and sort of parallel to the body, requires less effort on the part of the arm than with the other methods. The moment of inertia of the racquet is much less than when it is held out and rotated back with the body in the classic method, or pivoted up and back with the loop method. Also, pulling the racquet back with the head lagging just happens to be an easier task for the muscles than taking the racquet back head first.

A subtle but very good byproduct of the loop method is that it is conducive to the use of a relaxed arm and wrist. Another side benefit is that as the arm and racquet are pulled along the shoulder and body are pulled around too into what can become a rather exemplary ready position. Not taking the shoulder back by that or other means limits the length of racquet travel in the forward direction and the development of arm, shoulder, and racquet momentum.

TIMING ADJUSTMENTS

With the loop or leading elbow methods the racquet head gets back just in time instead of ahead of time, and it is easy to get caught with the racquet being a little late going into the forward swing. However it also happens not to be difficult to compensate for such lateness because the racquet can be easily slowed down or speeded up to adjust the timing. The reasons for this are that momentum has not been lost, a fair amount of reserve arm strength is available with these methods, and the moment of inertia to be overcome is minimized because of the small radius of the arc.

With the classic straight backswing the timing can be just as accurate and the adjustments reasonably easy if the racquet is taken back early and the forward swing is started in time. But the problem with many players is that the timing tends to be late or at least marginally so, and when that habit exists with the classic swing the lateness is accentuated as tiredness sets in. One means of reducing lateness is by visualizing the backswing as part of the process of developing momentum in the forward swing.

A fairly common exaggeration of the backswing is in taking the racquet back too far. This complicates the timing problems just by reason of the extra long intervals required for both the backswing and the forward swing. In some cases, such as for desperation shots and for high bounces, there is the opposite and more undesirable exaggeration of not taking a long enough backswing.

Taking the racquet back an added measure has a use when it is desired to hit the ball very hard. The momentum can be built up more easily in the forward swing over the lengthened distance, while the timing of the forward swing is hardly changed thereby. This timing consideration is described more fully in the chapter on "BLASTING."

RECEIVING FAST BALLS

The backswing used for a particular shot depends not only on preferences but circumstances. Many expert players automatically resort to whatever backswing is appropriate for the type of shot and the exigencies of the situation. For instance, the first half of the classic method (the quarter turn of the body) is commonly used when receiving very fast serves because, whatever the pros and cons for that backswing, it can be safely abbreviated since the racquet can always be kept properly faced for the hit.

So when a serve arrives unexpectedly fast the backswing can be cut short and the racquet brought forward with the proper attitude, and with whatever momentum has been generated by the time the ball zooms into the hitting zone. Not much racquet momentum is necessary or even desirable in this case because the momentum of the oncoming ball can be reused. That topic is discussed in the chapters on "ELASTICITY" and "INSECURITY." A slow moving racquet also has the advantage of providing better control, especially when an angled return is desired.

chapter fourteen hitting with the elbow bent

Why hit with a bent elbow? Or why not? "Hit" is emphasized because the elbow is bound to be bent to a varying extent during parts of the swing before and after the hit. But during the actual hit should the elbow be bent or shouldn't it? The classic instruction in this regard is that the elbow should be rather straight but not awkwardly so, and this seems to be rather good advice. However, there is no consensus view on that point and many pros do hit with somewhat more of a bent elbow than seems proper, not necessarily always wisely.

TECHNICAL CONSIDERATIONS

Some of the effects of a bent elbow are that the radius and the arc of the swing are shortened, and the "moment of inertia" of the racquet reduced. The moment of inertia has magnified importance because it is related not just to the distance of each particle from the center of rotation but to the square of that distance.

The lowered inertial factor and the greater strength of the arm close in compared with when it is more fully extended ease the job of developing rotational velocity in the arm and racquet. Other consequences are that the disguise of the direction of the hit can be accomplished relatively easily and that the interval of the swing is shortened. The latter effect creates an advantage somewhat akin to that obtained when taking the ball on the rise. An unobservant receiver may find the ball returning not faster but yet a little sooner than expected.

ANGULAR VELOCITY vs. FORWARD VELOCITY

Players instinctively associate the quick rotation obtained with a bent elbow as synonymous with added pace on the ball. So when extra pace is desired it is very common for players, even at the top levels, to hit with the elbow pulled in considerably more than on a normal stroke. But being able to swing the racquet around quickly in an angular sense doesn't necessarily equate to more racquet velocity, especially not in the direction of the hit.

A large angular velocity with a short radius is not likely to produce a forward speed of the racquet head that is any greater than that obtained with less angular velocity but a longer radius. The advantage, except for the factor of the strength of the arm being greater close in, is probably with the more extended arm. The arc of the swing is proportional to six times the radius. So it is difficult to improve on the racquet momentum generated with a comfortably extended arm.

DISADVANTAGES

One of the drawbacks of a bent elbow is that it is conducive to shortening the follow-through. While this permits quick readiness for the return it can seriously diminish the recovery of energy by compromising the period of contact and by introducing roundhouse. An added disadvantage is that it requires a sudden exertion that usually takes up all the strength of the arm, leaving nothing in reserve even though there is more of it available initially than with an extended arm.

Consequently the arm is likely to become overloaded at the hit, and is then at a disadvantage in countering the momentum of the ball. This inadequacy is aggravated by the fact that the resistance presented to the impact with a bent arm depends on muscular force, not on the more rigid reinforcement obtained through the bone structure of a more nearly straight arm angled somewhat forward against the shock.

THE QUASI BENT ELBOW SWING

If in the process of a swing the elbow is initially bent but is then gradually let out as the racquet approaches the hitting point, the extra strength of the arm with a close in elbow is available initially when it can be useful for a quick start up, while a long radius and arc of swing are available later on when needed to optimize racquet momentum and the storage and recovery of energy.

Properly used this combination of the properties of two types of swings can produce exceptional pace. Thus although more skills must be mastered with this more complicated technique there are advantages that can be gained. Many lower level players tend to do the opposite: hold the arm out initially and then draw the elbow further in as the stroke progresses.

TIMING CONSIDERATIONS

One of the considerations in regard to a bent elbow is whether it is to be used on all strokes of a type, all forehands say, or just some. If only on some there will be variation in the durations of swings due to the mentioned different angular velocities. Therefor when the elbow is brought in closer than normal the swing should usually be made to start a little later than with a more nearly straight arm, or else the racquet will usually reach the intended hitting point a little before the ball gets there. Such problems arise mainly when there is inadvertent change, or even a required change due to an emergency situation.

The amount of bend in the elbow is not easily kept constant, and the variations become more pronounced as tiredness sets in and the player fails to get properly into position for every shot. Any variation introduces changes in the length of the arc, the direction in which the racquet faces, the angular velocity, the interval, and therefore the internal and external timing. The associated changes may be small, but a very small error at the racquet can mean a sizable error when the ball gets to the other end of the court. On the positive side, because of the more instantaneous nature of a compact swing it is in fact easier to accommodate bad bounces and to time the exact instant of a hit with a short arc than with a long, smooth swing.

Although mere awareness of the effects of the variation on the timing will trigger some automatic adjustment, even then the net result will still be an additional propensity toward an erratic game. Naturally it is more likely that inexpert players will not make the appropriate changes in timing than that they will have enough knowledge and expertise to make the suitable finely tuned adjustments. Of course if a very consistent bend is always used then there is little variation in timing to contend with.

Average players time the forward swing mostly on the basis of the ball's position, and with not enough account of its speed. When the ball arrives sooner than expected one of the few available last instant adjustments is to bring the elbow in so as to be able to sweep the racquet around extra quickly, and by that means manage to meet the ball somewhat properly. The bent elbow swing is made to order for such an emergency. But a disadvantage is that repeated use as an expedient may rapidly fix it as a permanent habit.

TIMING THE LONG SWING

A long swing is graceful and effective but raises the risk of problems inherent with early commitment. There is an extended period of racquet travel during which the ball can bounce unpredictably, be affected by the wind or spin, etc. It takes skill and confidence to risk the difficult timing associated with an early start and a long swing interval. Nevertheless, instead of something to be avoided, early commitment is something of an accomplishment because it promotes proper preparation, good development of momentum, close attention to timing, and smooth execution.

Inexpert players are more apt than the proficient to avoid the challenges inherent in a long swing. They generally seek the feeling of security of a late swing with a very short arc obtained with an exaggeratedly bent elbow. But even the better players tend to shorten the swing when their confidence begins to waver during a difficult match. The qualms may be excusable where timing problems arise from such factors as a bad court surface, fading daylight, or windy conditions.

But if they occur just because of a loss of confidence then the trust placed in a quicker swing with a reduced arc usually turns out to be misplaced.

PROBLEMS OF DIRECTION

For a ball hit at a point in line with say the "net" foot (nearest the net), a racquet moving in a small arc is at a greater angle to the net than a racquet travelling in a larger arc. Therefor the use of the small arc may require that the wrist be bent back slightly to keep the racquet facing in the desired forward direction at the hit.

The racquet veers quickly into roundhouse with a short arc even when care is taken to see to it that a normal hitting point is used. Therefor when using a bent elbow it is necessary to make sure that there is an adequate follow-through in the intended direction of the ball. Such refinements to the termination can cause the bent elbow swing to resemble the quasi bent elbow stroke mentioned a little earlier, in which the arm is gradually unbent so as to be almost extended at contact.

CENTRIPETAL EFFORT TO OPPOSE CENTRIFUGAL FORCE

There is a subtle but important problem of a completely different nature with the use of a bent elbow. A swing is basically a section of a circle, or at least partly so, and the body is at the center. Therefor as the racquet and the arm develop momentum some of it is centrifugal, pulling outward on the arm. If the arm is comfortably extended the outward pull is merely taken up by the arm structure with no need for any significant amount of muscular effort.

However if the elbow is bent then the outward pull of the centrifugal force tries to straighten the elbow. Unfortunately, unlike with inertia, the pull is greater with a shorter radius than with a long. Muscular effort must be exerted to resist the pull and keep the elbow held in toward the body. Players are probably all too conscious of the resultant unpleasant feel and the tiring effect on the arm, but few are specifically aware of its cause. Such feelings seem to most people to be just the unavoidable attributes of the process of swinging the racquet, rather than the result of the self imposed task of continually restraining the arm and the racquet inward.

Allowing the elbow to gradually straighten during the swing transfers the centrifugal tension to the arm structure, reduces the demands on the muscles, and enhances acceleration of the racquet and the length of the follow-through. The opposite is true when the elbow is pulled closer in, as many players impulsively do when trying to hit extra hard.

The above theories are not idle conjectures but issues of significant import, and they illustrate how unexpected major consequences of slight variations in technique remain mysteries if the understandings depend completely on intuitive associations without inclusion of at least a smattering of technical knowledge. While tennis is only a game it cannot repeal or disregard the principles of physics.

Notes on

144

chapter fifteen
wrist flex and the grip

For expert players the wrist simply seems to do whatever is appropriate for a particular hit. A description of what actually happens that is simple enough to be put into words runs the risk of being skeletonized enough to border on the ambiguous and even misleading. Substantial wrist action is a requirement on serves, but is more a matter of personal choice on ground strokes. It is another variable to master, but when used properly it has advantages that are ample reward for the trouble of learning the skill.

SQUEEZE THE GRIP?

Tennis books have been quite limited as to descriptions of how to use wrist action. A traditional bit of contrary advice is to squeeze the grip at impact. This is not very compatible with a flexible wrist, if that happens to be what a person wishes to use. An ambiguity about "squeeze the grip" is whether or not there is some definite amount of pressure that is optimum. If so then only people with relatively weak muscles would be candidates for its use since a strong person's "loose" grip is apt to be much more firm than a weak person's "tight."

The grip need only be firm enough to enable application of the increments of force necessary to maintain a gradual acceleration, and to form a path for reinforcing the racquet with the arm and the body in countering the impact of the ball. The firmness of grip suitable for these purposes should largely suffice to overcome the torque generated by tolerably off center hits also.

A variable that affects the amount of pressure required is the degree of slipperiness of the racquet handle. Slippery handles can introduce awkwardness and unnaturalness by causing uncharacteristic tension in the arm muscles, making the wrist and arm undesirably stiff. This can cause serious deterioration in a person's game.

There is a greater danger of using too stiff a wrist than too loose. Therefor when a firmer grip than what is being used is desirable a more ambiguous advice than "squeeze the grip" might be in order. This can be done by reference to the task rather than the technique: improving on the intents of the hit, accelerating the racquet into the follow-through, getting the body weight and motion into the shot, etc.

If the momentum of the racquet is commonly inadequate then the player is likely to have learned to squeeze the grip fairly tightly in order to substitute strength for racquet momentum in countering the impact of the ball. Most of the force exerted by an oncoming ball is taken up by the elasticities, but a part is taken up in simply slowing the velocity of the racquet. That velocity will be less than zero (the racquet will get pushed backward) if the force developed by the combination of racquet momentum and physical strength is not at least equal to the force developed by the momentum of the ball.

On a well executed swing the racquet momentum will carry the racquet through the ball without the need for the application of much additional strength. With poor stroke production, or when there is a mis-hit, the racquet must be gripped very tightly to prevent the racquet from being knocked out of place in the hand. On a serve the racquet has to contend only with the inertia of the ball, not any initial momentum. So the grip for the serve can be very loose, and wrist flex can be used to maximum advantage in increasing racquet and ball velocities.

COMPENSATIONS WITH THE GRIP

If a hit is off center toward either edge of the racquet a compensating tightening of the grip will occur as soon as the torque generated by the hit begins to be transmitted to the hand. The tightening of the grip will be an automatic response, not a consciously controlled action. For a person to focus attention on that detail is apt to amount to overcompensation, and to be detrimental to the larger objective of doing the many other things that are necessary for a good hit.

An association that should not be suggested or implied is that the turning of the racquet in the hand is the result of looseness in the grip. That turning is more validly related to off center hits, and should be corrected in that respect rather than merely alleviated by means of a firmer grip. In fact, switching to a looser than normal grip can be of help in such cases. Correcting the real flaw, the off center hit, will then be the only available means to minimize torque, turning of the racquet, and misdirection of the ball. An exaggeratedly loose grip can also be deliberately used, at least during practice, to begin to eliminate other bad features such as pushing, bad timing, slowing of the swing, improper hitting point, etc.

MINIMIZING SHOCK

With a loose grip the jolt of the impact has no solid path of transmission from racquet to arm. For that reason, and because it doesn't lend itself to the use of strength as a replacement for racquet momentum, or the use of compensations for improper timing and techniques, a loose grip can facilitate getting rid of tennis elbow.

In some respects a sore arm or wrist can act as a training aid in learning how to hit with minimal strain and effort. An increase in pain will be an instant warning of bad execution, while a much less noticeable level of pain will be an indication of a corresponding improvement in the techniques. However it is quite unwise to hit if pain is being experienced. Permanent damage could result.

On the other hand, if a player is going to play a match in spite of some minor injury to the arm then the use of a loose grip may be advisable as a means of minimizing added damage. At the same time the loose grip may make it possible to stay competitive in the match by forcing the use of the better techniques. But any shot for which adequate racquet momentum cannot be attained should not be attempted when playing with injuries. There would be a considerable danger of increasing the severity of the damage, and the shot would probably result in a setup or an error anyway.

USING THE WRIST FOR CONTROL AND POWER

Most players feel more in control of the racquet and the ball with a firm wrist than with the flexible. However, the entire arm has to get involved when a last instant change has to be made with a firm wrist. The same correction can often be achieved more easily with the wrist alone if the wrist is loose. Wrist action is quicker, more flexible, and more precise than that of the entire arm, besides still retaining all the possibilities of moving the arm as required also.

Another potential advantage of wrist flex is power. Whatever velocity is obtained in the racquet due to wrist flex adds directly and considerably to the velocity of the racquet due to the swing of the arm and the movement of the body. The velocity contributed by the flex is additive to that obtained from the swing, sort of a miniature swing hinged at the wrist added to the larger swings hinged at the elbow and shoulder.

The distance of the wrist to the center of the racquet head is roughly about twenty inches. This constitutes the radius of the arc of racquet head travel created by wrist flex. The distance of the wrist to the center of the hand is only about two or three inches. So the velocity of the racquet head due to wrist flex can be as much as ten times that developed in the hand by the same flex.

UNWISE USE OF FLEX

The caution here, as usual, is that the advantage of extra power should not be the cause of going overboard. If flex is used immoderately the benefits are apt to be cancelled by distortions induced in other elements of the stroke. Flex should be obtained only as it occurs naturally in a good hit, and not as an exaggerated flourish in itself.

Trying for more than is appropriate also means that the strength of the wrist will be over utilized, with none left to counter the impact of the ball. Although the muscles of the wrist have the advantage of the·mentioned multiplication factor in converting wrist flex to racquet velocity, they suffer that same factor as a disadvantage in the magnification of the shock created by the impact of the ball.

An additional hazard with the use of flex is that if the ball arrives before the racquet has been given a good start in the forward direction the wrist can be caught when it is both heavily stressed and is also in a very vulnerable position. Damage can result. The use of wrist flex is therefore somewhat inadvisable on balls that approach extra fast, especially since on such balls it is quite easy to misjudge and be tardy in the timing. On the other hand, if the flex happens to be timed exactly correctly the added racquet momentum created by the wrist flex can reduce the normal shock of impact correspondingly.

BLOCKING THE BALL BACK

Another example of misuse of wrist flex is the tendency of many inexpert players to swing from the wrist on volleys. Besides being ineffective this happens to be most cruel punishment for the wrist. The shot should normally be hit by blocking the ball back and adding a little bit of shove. The shove is usually referred to as a punch, but that seems to be a somewhat exaggerated description of what actually occurs. It is more like moving the hand forward when catching a light ball than shooting the hand forward to inflict a blow. While the wrist is not completely locked for the volley only a minor element of flex is generally involved.

The player who tries to swing at the volley is under the misconception that the ball will not have much pace unless delivered to it by the racquet. On the contrary, just blocking the ball back with a firm wrist can provide surprising power since the opponent's passing shots will usually be hit very hard. If the ball is a floater then a swing may be justified, and the stroke can justifiably be quite wristy. The use of flex is an ideal method for adding extra pace on balls that sit up.

A strong person can get fairly good results with just the use of the strength of a stiff arm and wrist in a blocking type hit, minimizing the need to get into exactly the correct position for a conventional swing. Neither the ball nor the racquet are that heavy that it takes more than moderate physical strength, even with a short swing, to develop both reasonable momentum in the racquet and reinforcement with the body more than sufficient to counteract the impact of the ball. Yet the ball is heavy enough so that its impact can be quite unpleasant if the arm is caught unprepared.

Where the blocking type hit has its major advantages is in the minimum energy needed to get into a suitable position, in good visibility of the court during the entire shot, and in the feeling of security obtained from a stroke that is not long and complex but short and simple, and that moves in the direction of the hit. But while a push with the use of strength can be effective in preventing the racquet from being knocked back by the ball, and while a firm racquet means efficient storage of the energy existing in the ball, there is inefficiency in the recovery process and little contribution of new energy to the shot via racquet momentum.

CONSERVING ENERGY

Older players have other reasons for using wrist flex. As the eyes weaken and the reflexes, coordination, timing, and mobility fade, the long strokes may get to be beyond physical capabilities. The need to minimize the use of strength dictates that the body be placed closer to the path of the ball, and the hitting point be moved more forward than what would be considered optimum.

The change need not mean progressive deterioration. The compactness of the strokes allows a decent level of play when long free swings become quite impractical. That is probably the reason why the short chop stroke finds so much favor among seniors, and in truth works quite well.

The chop gives good racquet acceleration at the right time; good reinforcement with the shoulder; not much arm motion but all of it directed into the hit (except as used for spin); ease of use with an open stance (which minimizes the amount of movement between the waiting and hitting positions); good visibility of the ball, the hitting point, the court, and the opponent; easy switch from deep hits to drop shots; ease of making last instant adjustments for unexpected bounces; and easing of the eye and hand coordination requirements because of the short swing and because most of the action is in front in the field of vision.

The demands on the strength are usually further minimized by the racquet moving from high to low as it comes forward. Gravity thus helps out in generating the racquet velocity sufficient for a good hit. The elbow is held close to the body, so the moment of inertia of the racquet is low. The chop does sacrifice pace, but the flex of the wrist can partially make up. Also, in an absolute sense the senior game does not depend on heavy pace anyhow.

Underspin is a natural product because of the downward travel of the racquet. The spin is effective in enhancing control because balls with underspin tend not to drop but to keep moving in a straight line, thus making it easier to judge the aim. On the negative side, the spin tends to make the ball sit up at the bounce and invite an offensive return. When seniors carry the use of underspin to the extreme of making frequent drop shots against players who cannot move well then in most cases nobody really wins because there is little likelihood of extended exchanges with solid, satisfying hits.

Notes on

chapter sixteen

blasting

There is no one term that is the consensus choice to describe the means used to hit the ball as hard as possible. The subject has not even been one of the standard topics of instruction. In this book the process will be called "blasting," not out of any real preference but to avoid the confusion created with the use of a multiplicity of terms for the same thing. Other words that could just as easily be used are "slug," "smash," and "wallop." More descriptive terms include "go for a winner," "go all out," "cream the ball," and "go for it," but these are too cumbersome to be used with any frequency.

WHEN TO BLAST

Many tournament players consistently hit the ball very hard, but few go all out for winners more than very occasionally because at tournament level nobody can afford to make any extra errors. Very few coaches would recommend trying to blast on every shot, while some advocate that it should never be done.

A well thought out example of the latter type of advice is that the player should approach each and every shot with the intention of winning the point not on that hit but on the one after. This means that even on strokes that are hit with extra pace the intention should be to hit a forcing shot instead of an outright winner. The object is to keep the opponent under pressure so as to ultimately force either an outright error or a setup that can easily be put away.

WAYS OF BLASTING

The means for getting maximum pace can be arbitrarily assigned into five major categories as follows: intensify the physical effort, conserve racquet momentum, improve the length and timing of the swing, augment the swing of the arm with body motion and wrist and arm flex, and improve and lengthen the contact interval.

These categories have been arbitrarily selected just for this discussion as a means of organizing and bringing to the attention what seem to be the most important ideas. It is not claimed that the categories are either all inclusive or exclusive, or that other breakdowns would not work just as well. Within them, but sometimes spanning across several of them, are the specific techniques for generating extra power.

One way that effort can be intensified is through increased firmness in the arm and wrist to prevent the racquet from being knocked backward by the impact of the approaching ball. This technique is well suited for balls that approach with a great deal of pace. There are negative aspects to the method in that such firmness inhibits the use of wrist and arm flex to generate added power, and in that the application of an extra amount of strength could cause the stroke to become more like a push than a swing.

In fact an increase in power can often be obtained by the contrary method of keeping the muscles loose, especially those of the shoulder, even while also trying to apply extra strength. A way to bring about a balance between use of strength and looseness of muscles is to think in terms of getting the body wound up to send the weight of the racquet into and through the ball. The effectiveness here is obtained mostly through better development and use of racquet momentum.

Another way to apply more effort is to increase the acceleration and velocity of the arm, either by the use of greater force or the same force over a bigger arc and a longer period of time. The arc can be made large by extending the arm or increasing the amount of body motion. An alternate method of lengthening the time and space intervals is to increase the length of the backswing. This lengthens the forward swing correspondingly.

A different approach is to preserve the racquet momentum generated in the backswing by carrying it into the forward swing via a looped path. Enlarging the size of the loop, but not to the point of exaggeration, may help also. The continuous curved path provides conservation of racquet momentum, while increasing the size of the loop gives added time and space over which to accelerate the racquet.

A very important increase in the pace of the ball can be obtained through the use of wrist and arm flex. It was shown in the previous chapter that a flex at the wrist can result in an increase in racquet velocity that can be ten times that developed in the hand by the same flex. Similarly, arm flex obtained via a swing hinged at the elbow can also augment racquet velocity. Both the flex at the wrist and at the elbow add to the velocity generated by the swing of the arm as hinged at the shoulder.

TIMING COMPLICATIONS

A complication introduced by a swing that is faster than normal is that the time interval of the swing is shortened. In effect the ball is a little late in arriving. So the racquet will reach the location of the preferred hitting point a little sooner than the ball, resulting in the actual hitting point being a little forward of the normal.

The shift of the hitting point forward from the optimum will cause a loss of pace in the ball instead of the intended enhancement. The negative reward may then lead the player to use ever more compulsive efforts on succeeding shots instead of making the obvious adjustment of correcting the timing of the swing. This can be done by delaying the start of the forward swing a minute amount or by lengthening the swing a trifle.

There is an obscure complicating factor involved in the effort to swing faster: it is desired to build up more racquet velocity than normal, but to the extent that this is actually accomplished the time interval available to do it in has been correspondingly reduced to less than normal. This factor tends to diminish the rewards for the trouble. A normal interval is largely preserved when the faster swing is obtained with wrist flex, since arm speed is not increased and since the initially laid back wrist lengthens the path of the swing.

INVOLVEMENT OF THE BODY

Increasing the forward shift of the body, or stepping into the hit, or increasing the rotation of the body when it is carrying the shoulder forward and not sideways, can all add appreciably to racquet velocity. Although these particular methods increase racquet velocity, which advances the hitting point by cutting down on the time interval of the swing, they also move the body toward the hitting point, and this effectively is the same as moving the hitting point backward.

So as far as the hitting point is concerned the effect of moving the body into the shot is opposite to that obtained by swinging the racquet faster. If a faster arm swing and increased forward movement of the body are both used then the time variations tend to cancel. Which effect will dominate depends on the particular combination of internal and external timing used. Obviously an improper mix of such actions can create unexpected results.

If there is a slowing of the swing and also a greater than normal forward movement of the body the resultant problems are additive because both actions cause the swing to be late with respect to the arrival of the ball. Conversely, a faster swing and less than normal movement of the body are additive in causing the swing to be early. In either case a bad error could result, and the player would probably not have a good idea as to why it happened. These are ideas that should have some control over the intents for the shot but not conscious control of the execution. They could help to explain some types of errors, and could minimize misconceptions or false assignment of errors.

The complications associated with variations in the movement of the body and the swing of the arm illustrate the fact that when something special is being attempted all required changes to subsidiary actions must be taken care of. If they are not it may be of worse than no use to try to do the something special. Little factors not accounted for can equate to big errors.

Some of the best players can be seen making inexcusable errors because of a lack of finesse in a few fine areas such as those just discussed. The adjustments cannot be calculated and must occur entirely automatically. For a skilled player they usually do, but when they do not "unexplainable" errors may occur that are not correctable by such usual remedies as "watching the ball." Timing complications help to account for the fact that many attempts at blasting end up as points for the opponent.

BODY ROTATION

With the rotational type of motion inherent in a turn of the torso, and a certain amount is not only unavoidable but useful in all shots, a big danger is that the body can easily rotate ahead of the arm, breaking the reinforcement with the body. Care should also be taken to have the swing flatten out and go mostly forward in the area of the hitting point, not degenerate into roundhouse.

Many players take a more sideways position than usual in preparing for an all out effort, or may just turn the torso back an extra degree, or both. The more sideways attitude helps make an increase in the length of the swing possible. This will help to develop added racquet momentum and at the same will offset the need to slow the timing to accommodate the faster swing. But almost nothing is simple and few rules are fast. As discussed under "THE OPEN STANCE" in the chapter on "FOOTWORK," extra power can be obtained with that stance by initially placing the torso in tension via a strong twist of the body.

Some very successful pros hit with less of a sideways stance and less movement of the body and shoulder than would seem to be sufficient. The apparent motives, besides a desire to look where the ball is going and to loaf like anybody else, are to optimize the view of the ball and the other side of the court, and to keep the body out of the way of the arm on the forehand. As important as it is to employ the most effective hitting techniques it must be recognized that there are other objectives that could take precedence under some circumstances.

THE IMPORTANCE OF THE CONTACT INTERVAL

A most important consideration that may not get the attention required on attempts at blasting is the length of the contact interval. The traditional instructions relating to that subject on any stroke are to "hold the ball on the racquet as long as possible," and to "follow-through in the direction of the shot."

But, while both ideas are valid, the first implies maintaining the forward travel of the racquet further than may be necessary or practical, and the second doesn't mention other factors without which the follow-through is just a rather useless gesture. The principal means of controlling the length of the contact interval are to develop adequate racquet momentum, accelerate the racquet through contact, maintain racquet travel in the direction of the hit during contact, and reinforce the racquet and the arm with the body. The push and the quick slap do not fulfill those reuirements and are not effective means of blasting.

Disregard of the requirements related to lengthening the contact interval has negative consequences on the storage and recovery of energy. For that reason a player's most impulsive efforts may not produce a particularly fast paced ball, while a long, relaxed swing in the direction of the shot, with enough reserve strength to counter the impact and provide good acceleration during contact, may with seemingly only moderate effort produce a bullet.

The mentioned definitions of the means of getting extra power (use extra effort, conserve momentum, lengthen and improve the timing of the swing, augment the motion of the arm with other motions, and improve and lengthen contact) can be employed either largely individually or in combinations, mostly the latter. A list of the more specific characteristics of good blasting would include a considerably more extensive preparation than on a normal drive. Any attempt to exploit any means that happens to be already optimally exploited will yield negative results.

INDIVIDUAL STYLES OF BLASTING

Any of the techniques may be given special emphasis at the expense of the others. This imbalance does usually happen and need not be detrimental. For instance, if the elbow is brought in for a swing with a shortened arc, which is usually considered undesirable, there can be benefits in the form of reduced racquet inertia and increased arm strength. An important additional factor is that the bend of the elbow makes it possible to employ the previously mentioned arm flex.

So, properly put together, the overall result of a close-in, bent elbow swing can be a substantial gain in power. This general type of technique is in fact used by most, but not all, of the top players who blast frequently and well. The general style and the amount of extension of the arm tend to be very individualistic, and the people who do blast successfully are their own best advisors as to which technique works best for them.

While it is true that quite a few tournament players consistently shorten the swing by bringing the arm in toward the body when trying to hit extra hard, whether or not this really provides an advantage over other possible methods is another matter. There is a danger of bringing the elbow in just because of a feeling of weakness and artificiality when the arm is extended. The short swing and short time interval give the impression of high racquet velocity, but this could be just an illusion. Perhaps, given the same extra involvement of the body, a long swing with an almost extended arm might do even better.

The question may be raised that since the mentioned bent elbow technique for blasting seems to be quite popular and successful why not use it all the time? The main reasons why not are an increase in the rate of error, a disadvantage in terms of reach, a high expenditure of energy, increased strain on the arm and shoulder muscles, and less pace rather than more if the ball is not set up approximately right for the purpose.

Conscious individual application of any of the mentioned means of getting increased pace may cause those techniques to be unnatural, exaggerated, and self defeating. The proper techniques and the proper intensity come out of an intent to hit for effect with a feeling for how to do it, and with the involvement of the body in a full and free expression of that intent. It is not effective to attempt to superimpose selected details onto an existing style.

THE EFFECTS OF WRONG INTENTIONS

Blasting has a tendency to bring out the worst habits in a player. The methods brought into use quite often involve violent but abbreviated effort, body ahead of arm, muscling rather than stroking, poor reinforcement with the body, a circular rather than forward swing of the racquet, jumping and turning instead of moving the body into the shot, an unpredictable racquet angle at contact, hitting early, hitting with extravagant initial effort instead of maintaining a sufficient reserve, not adjusting for the timing variations involved, etc.

The quite normal urge of wanting more than is obtainable with legitimate means triggers the use of the unworkable. The often misguided intent is as if to discard the proper hitting techniques and sort of create an explosion at contact intended to send a weightless ball instantaneously to the furthest quarter inch of the court. Since these attempts involve a fantasy land type concept of the nature of the physical processes, and of the chances of hitting that last quarter of an inch, the real world results are likely to be an unsatisfactory pace and an enormously increased rate of error.

Some players are motivated to blast not by a feeling of super competence but by a subconscious feeling of not being capable of really "earning" a point or sustaining a rally. They therefore find it necessary to try for a lucky and spectacular winner instead. The fact that there is no rationality in the technique used, that the feel of the hit is very unpleasant, the error rate multiplied, energy used at an excessive rate, and the pace of the ball not at all augmented as expected, does not deter the continual use of impractical means in the pursuit of unrealistic results.

A disappointing pace is apt to cause a player to choose the irrational solution of trying to do even more than what already proved to be unattainable: untouchable passing shots, impossible angles, line drives intended to pass right through the opponent, balls that barely clear the net and land right on the base line, balls aimed at a point impossibly close behind the net, drop shots intended to reach the net and then slide down the other side, getting set to hit in one direction but then hitting in a completely different direction, etc., all with unsuitable techniques. One lucky success appears to justify any number of ignominious failures. Unfortunately for such intents, lucky shots occur unpredictably and only occasionally for anybody at any level of play.

THE MISUSE OF ENERGY

A common illusion is the idea that a violent effort guarantees a sensational result, a placing of faith in the savageness of the force instead of the appropriateness of the technique. The association is not entirely irrational since it is logical to believe that if good results can be obtained with moderate effort it should be possible to get fantastic results with extravagant effort. But the energy expended and shock experienced do not in fact correlate to the best utilization of the characteristics of elasticity.

Since effective hitting is not in actuality the consequence of a great amount of strain and shock, the extra exertion is in some ways akin to the attempts of motorists to blow the horn louder by jamming down harder on the horn button. At least the horn behaves the same in any case, no better or no worse, while in tennis the consequence may be exactly counter to the intention.

A frequent motive for the use of all out effort, especially on setups where it is not really needed, is the feeling that an extra hard hit is somehow that much more painful to the opponent. But the opposite is true since an increase in the error rate is inevitable, and easy setups get converted into disastrous errors. The heavy expenditure of energy is in itself a very high price to pay for an unnecessary display of power, even without the unaffordable loss of points on improbable errors. And even if the blast is impressively successful it does not provide any bonus points.

EMOTIONAL EXERTION

Extra emotional effort causes the tensing of a great many muscles that have no useful function in the stroke and so would ordinarily be idle. The extravagant use of normally uninvolved muscles actually interferes with the mechanics of the shot in addition to wasting huge amounts of energy. Allowing the emotions to run wild prevents adequate concentration on the intentions, preparation, and execution.

Some players engage in outbursts that arouse resentment in the opponent, motivating that person to resort to the above described emotional exertion. It is too much to expect that people under heavy stress and exertion will always refrain from engaging in disruptive behavior over real, imagined, trivial, or even fictitious problems. But where it is only the other player who then hits shots in anger the outbursts are at best inconsiderate, and at worst may be unfair tactics.

The trick for the victim of such tactics is to feel thankful for the extra time available to recuperate, analyze problems, restore a feel of rhythm, review strategy, decide on the means to improve execution, use slow motion visualization, etc. At the same time the agitator is otherwise engaged and is not similarly benefited. When the tactics are deliberate the biggest disappointment for the perpetrator could be the realization that the plot did not work and may even have backfired.

INTELLIGENT BLASTING

In spite of the problems and risks involved with blasting, the probable trend in the future will be toward greater use of attempts to blast the ball past the opponent whenever a suitable bounce occurs, rather than just playing it safe at all times. In the future the question will probably not be who blasts and who doesn't, but who blasts better and more intelligently?

Fortunately the principles outlined as necessary to the proper execution of the standard strokes are also those that are the key to getting maximum results out of blasting. Making the best use of elasticity imparts the best velocity. The pattern for blasting may not look like that of a standard stroke but the principles of elasticity, acceleration, reinforcement, recovery of energy, etc. have to get the same consideration, and even more. The more speed desired the more necessary to obey the basic principles.

The power stroke should still be hit with control, not with an emotional, wild swing above the capabilities of the body or the responses of the equipment. The objectives of the swing can change but not the basic concepts of a hit, otherwise the player will abandon most of what is productive to revert back to satisfying emotional urges and paying the inevitable penalties.

Extreme pace is best used only when it can be useful and the ball is set up just right. Its use is not advisable when the opponent doesn't stand a chance of getting to the ball even if it is given only moderate pace. There is no profit in hitting with reckless violence and the substantial possibility of an inexcusable error, and letting the opponent enjoy a monopoly on the use of the legitimate methods of enhancing velocity.

BLASTING OFF OF LOW BOUNCES

An interesting phenomenon that can be put to good use in blasting is that a ball can ordinarily be hit harder off a low bounce than a normal bounce. Some of the possible factors are automatic nearly full extension of the arm, a longer swing, automatic positioning of the arm for good reinforcement, involvement of additional sets of muscles because of the need to hit up as well as forward, and the equivalent of added momentum in the approaching ball in the form of the pull of gravity.

However, if a ball is hit from a low position there is a big danger of sending it long because the hit has to have an upward slant. So topspin is advisable. But when energy is diverted into creating spin it takes away from pace. The trick is to optimize not maximize the spin, unless the extra high bounce is desired that comes with high spin. The objective in blasting is usually speed, not bounce. So the spin should usually be moderate since it doesn't take much to bring even a hard hit ball down within bounds.

If a player doesn't happen to understand intuitively the subtle ways to get extra pace, and also is not aware of the physical laws involved, then various brute force expedients, such as a quick, overpowering turn of the body, are often used as substitutes. The urge to use wrong techniques to try to achieve devastating velocity is not restricted to the dubs. Even in major tournaments it sometimes happens that top players blow very important setup shots by resorting to the most obviously inappropriate ways to try to slam a winner past the opponent.

chapter seventeen
the backhand

The discussions in the previous chapters were generally applicable to any stroke. What digression did occur was largely restricted to explaining a few special conditions, mostly on the forehand. It was therefore not necessary to skip back and forth between the main themes and the qualifications and exceptions. So part of the remaining task in the following chapters is to examine the special aspects of the other strokes. The backhand provides an area of particular interest and concern because of the problems it seems to present and the misunderstandings that are often involved.

While a well executed backhand is one of the finest and most graceful shots in tennis it is also a major source of frustration for a big majority of players. This is especially true for those who did not get instruction early but picked up both techniques and expedients on their own, consulting neither teachers nor texts for guidance.

The following discussion will pertain mostly to the classic one-handed backhand because it is a pattern to which the principal concepts can be conveniently related, and because it is felt, rightly or wrongly, that it is a particularly fine stroke. It should not be assumed, however, that a recommendation is implied as it being the one correct style for all players.

The mere fact that this discussion applies to a certain style constitutes somewhat of a departure from the general theme of this book: that it is not patterns but principles, intentions, experiences, and the satisfactions involved with hitting that should determine technique. That theme still holds, but in this case it is nevertheless not feasible to avoid focusing on a specific pattern.

THE SIDEWAYS STANCE

An important feature of the backhand is that the racquet arm for the one handed stroke is on the "net" side of the body rather than on the "fence" side. This circumstance limits the arm to a short backswing if a face-the-net stance is used. The arm then also lacks both strength and extension in the forward swing.

A sideways stance is almost mandatory on the classic backhand in order to eliminate interference from the body in the backswing and to make a fuller and freer stroke possible in the forward swing. So whereas on the forehand the stance is quite often partially open, on the classic backhand it is usually closed, even to the extent that the player's back can be somewhat turned toward the net.

A MORE FORWARD HITTING POINT

On both the forehand and backhand the hitting point must be slightly ahead of the racquet shoulder. This would seem to mean that the hitting point for the backhand should be the width of the body closer to the net than for the forehand, since on the forehand the racquet shoulder is on the "fence" side while on the backhand it is on the "net" side of the body.

However on the forehand the body turns forward somewhat during the stroke, while on the classic one-handed backhand the body is in a mostly sideways position through impact. So although the hitting point for the backhand is somewhat advanced compared with that for the forehand it is not by the full width of the body.

THE BACKHAND REACH

On the classic backhand the arm becomes remarkably free as it moves toward the hitting zone, whereas in the same area on the forehand the arm is restrained inward by the hitting shoulder. Therefore, unlike what happens on the forehand, the arm gets to be almost fully extended at the hit.

For that reason the player must stand a slightly greater distance away from the path of the ball than on the forehand. If this distance requirement is not met the closeness of the body to the path of the ball restricts the free flow of the swing, and the traditional difficulties which many players experience with the backhand begin to develop.

AN INITIAL OUTWARD ARC

Due to the above mentioned reversal of constraints the path of the racquet on the backhand differs in an important way from the standard concept of the racquet traveling forward in a rather straight line to meet the

171

ball. On the Eastern forehand the racquet travels more or less parallel to the body from the end of the backswing all the way through to the hit. This is not just by custom and intent.

The arm is strong in coming straight forward during the first half of the forehand and weak if it is extended to its full length at that time. Then in the second half of the swing the arm again cannot be extended freely because it is constrained inward by the body, as mentioned earlier. This latter situation is not true if an open stance is used, but in that case the arm has to be brought in for another reason: lack of strength when held out in the extended position.

On the backhand, by contrast, the arm is constrained inward at the end of the backswing but then becomes progressively more free in the forward swing until there are no restraints at all at the hit. Due to those circumstances the first task at the start of the forward swing is to move the arm out and away to get it to the comfortable extension that it should have on the approach to the hitting point.

So the racquet must initially circle somewhat outward toward the sideline before rounding the corner and moving forward in the direction of the hit. The arc is not an add-on detail, but is something that will occur naturally if the body position is sideways, the location of the hitting point is proper, and the arm is simply allowed to swing out and forward to that point. The outward arc is a free swing with an almost extended arm and can therefore generate good racquet velocity, especially if augmented with just a little wrist and elbow flex.

Without that initial arc the classic one-handed backhand tends to deteriorate into a push, deficient in acceleration and momentum, hard on the elbow, and costly in terms of the strength and energy required. Since one of the major advantages of the backhand is the availability of a long, unhindered swing it is undesirable to waste it with a push, or with other degenerate forms such as roundhouse, swipe, and slap.

INVOLVING THE IDLE HAND

A common recommendation regarding the one-handed swing is to support the racquet with both hands, at least by the end of the backswing. The second hand is then supposed to help start the racquet forward. The first part of this makes sense since the use of two hands can produce a more controlled ending to the backswing and can relieve the hitting arm of the weight and inertia of the racquet. However it is best to take the second hand off the handle at about the start of the forward swing. That hand prevents the racquet from travelling in a natural outward arc, and the racquet arm from going to the required comfortable near full extension.

RESEMBLANCE TO A BASEBALL SWING

In confirmation of the initial circular motion, the backhand has been compared by Don Budge[1], who is considered to have had one of the greatest classic style backhands of all time, to be similar to the swing of a baseball bat. However, because of the relatively great weight of a bat compared with that of a racquet, the final part of a baseball swing continues in more of a

---

1. "BOOK OF TENNIS" by the Editors of SPORTS ILLUSTRATED, p. 25, J.P. Lippincott Company

circle around the body than can be tolerated in tennis. Also, swinging a heavy bat forward results in a strong counter push created by the sizable inertia of the bat.

It is therefore not uncommon on a very hard swing in baseball to see the body being pushed backward, whereas it can and should be moving easily forward in similar circumstances in tennis. Even in baseball a forward motion of the body is just as desirable. Very hard swings that result in a noticeable backward move tend to cause the extra effort to be counterproductive.

The laws of elasticity and recovery of energy apply to baseball as to any act of hitting. This is true even though in baseball the contact interval is much shorter than in tennis due to the comparatively miniscule elasticities in both bat and ball. A moderately paced forward swing that will allow the body to move into the hit, rather than have it be pushed back, should provide the most power in baseball for the same reasons that it does in tennis.

THE ROUNDHOUSE BACKHAND

A few of the causes of the all too prevalent, wild, unpredictable, and unlovely roundhouse backhand are as follows: (1) The very correct classic backhand stroke starts forward naturally in a curved arc, and it easily happens that the curve is just continued rather than straightened out. (2) The player may not do enough about either getting the body ready initially, positioning it far enough from the path of the ball, or having it participate in the forward swing and the hit. (3) A turn to face the net may occur too soon. (4) The ball may be hit too early (too far toward the net), resulting in premature use of most of the available racquet travel in the forward direction. (5) Many players just resort to the expedient of swinging both the body and the arm around as suddenly as possible on the assumption that power is created thereby, or simply because they have not mastered a more proper swing.

THE OPEN STANCE

When a backhand is hit from an open stance the motion of the arm and racquet with respect to the body is something like the movement of the front blade of a pair of scissors. The backward and forward swings are both limited, and the angular travel of the racquet becomes more and more pronounced as it approaches the hitting point. Most of the forward movement at that location has to be forced, so the natural tendency is to pull the racquet sideways across the front of the body instead. The pull and the constantly changing angle of the racquet make it hard to control the direction of the hit.

Another action that is difficult from an open stance on the backhand is swinging upward. The arm is just not strong in that direction. An added problem is that the forward movement of the arm in front of the body is very restricted. A player using an open stance therefore generally allows the racquet to go down and to the side. Those actions are conducive to underspin, but a not very good variety in terms of effort expended, pace, accuracy, and control of spin. The same poor results are obtained even from a closed stance if the body and shoulder are rotated too far forward and around before or during the hit. In that case the upper body in effect operates out of an open stance regardless of where the feet may be.

The above criticisms do not apply to a properly executed underspin shot, and underspin is not undesirable per se. But here it is the inadvertent result of a cramped and deficient swing from an inappropriate position with little body participation, rather than a skillful stroke with its own special advantages.

THE BACKHAND TIMING DOES NOT MIRROR THE FOREHAND

Since the arm is relatively weak on the backhand and may be slow in gathering speed, and since the length of the forward swing is a little greater due to the mentioned factors of a rounded and more outward going initial arc, a more extended arm, and a more forward hitting point, it therefore happens that the elapsed time for the classic swing is likely to be a little greater than for the forehand.

The increase in the time is minuscule to be sure, but it may be enough to cause the ball to arrive a little early. This results in such things as a hurried stroke, wrong hitting point, incomplete development of momentum, damaging shock, and erratic control. Therefore the start of the forward swing must begin a little sooner than for a forehand. The timing interactions and complications that can arise out of such small variations are covered in the chapters on "TIMING" and "BLASTING."

While timing should be an automatic development of the stroke pattern, and while as a general rule players should not consciously and directly make timing compensations, it is useful to know that the timing of the elements of the backhand does not exactly parallel the same for the forehand. Without that knowledge a person may instinctively try to treat the two strokes as if they were mirror images of each other, which it is obvious they are not. The ultimate measure of correctness is the feel of a solid, momentum-powered hit.

A COLLECTION OF DIFFICULTIES

The mentioned timing differential, the unique nature of the arc of the swing, the positioning of the body further from the path of the ball, the relative weakness of the arm, and the advanced hitting point are probably the major reasons why players have unaccountable trouble in becoming completely comfortable with their backhands.

Feelings of insecurity due to lack of mastery of the more complicated pattern, difficulty with the timing of a long swing, and the special restrictions as to grip and stance are other factors that are sources of trouble. Nevertheless, the prevalence of problem backhands is probably caused more by bad habits acquired early than by the inherent complexities.

A major cause of degeneration on both the backhand and forehand is to progressively turn more toward the net too soon to look where the ball is intended to go. On the forehand this is not all bad if not already extreme because the arm is then made more free to move in the forward direction. On the backhand, however, the turn pulls the shoulder and the arm away from the hit. A powerless sideways swipe in front of the body results.

A PROBLEM WITH THE VIEW

Another difficulty with backhands is the poorer view of the court due to the very closed stance required. This is a special problem for players who wear glasses because the view of the ball on the backhand tends to be through the outside edge of the front lens (nearest the net). And the head must be turned decidedly forward to make even that possible.

177

Since light reflections from the skin onto the back surface of the lens increase in strength toward that same outside edge of the lens, the image of the ball will become dim and may actually disappear momentarily but totally behind the reflections. Players are ordinarily unaware of the interruption in the vision of the ball unless told about it, and are usually only subconsciously aware of any difficulty at all. The light from other sources besides the skin, such as from the eye, the surroundings, the sky, and especially the sun if it happens to be in a critical position, may also cause a similar interference.

The cure is to have the glasses made with an antireflective coating, as on camera lenses. The coatings are now more durable than at first, but any lenses, glass or plastic and coated or not, should be washed or at least rinsed to remove gritty dust before wiping.

On bright days some sort of visor is advisable because the light diffuses throughout the lenses, giving the effect of looking through a slight haze. Those players who find head wear uncomfortable or unbecoming may have less objection to miniature visors that shield only the glasses. These have the additional advantage of not interfering with the view of the ball on overheads.

USING TWO HANDS

The two-handed shot is a means to make up for the deficiency of strength in an extended arm. But the strength of two arms and a more solid reinforcement with the body are obtained at the expense of a freer swing, greater reach, and greater racquet momentum. Very few players also use a two-handed forehand because it is a "cross-handed" shot unless the hand positions are switched. When switching in that manner the player is really substituting a two-handed back-hand on the forehand side. Hand switching can be inconvenient during fast exchanges. There have been a few players, some right near the top, who hit great shots with a cross-handed grip.

The major disadvantage of any two-handed shot is loss of extension or reach. The main advantage is that the combined strength of the two hands makes it easi-er to maneuver the racquet. The two-handed swing gives strong acceleration in a short span of time and distance, little shock from impact, ease of learning, and ease of execution. These factors can help improve timing, control, manipulation, and disguise. For many players it can also mean improved pace.

But if the greater freedom, extension, and length of swing available on a one-handed shot are properly ex-ploited in developing racquet momentum then more pace should be obtainable thus than on the two-handed stroke. However the level of proficiency re-quired to hit the ball with heavy pace with the classic one-handed shot seems not to be easy to master, and particularly not for those people who started out with another style, or who acquired bad habits first.

AN UNCLASSICAL ALTERNATIVE

A one-handed backhand that is preferred by many play-ers nowadays is accomplished by using a straight for-ward push or fling of the racquet from a fully sideways position. While the results can be very good a strong arm is required, as well as considerable exertion. And the higher level of shock and strain can make repeated use a source of damage to the arm. The stroke is not at all a free swing since the body and shoulder positions are usually partially frozen rather than moved and rotated into the hit.

The body is positioned closer to the path of the ball for this shot than for the traditional stroke. There is therefore a loss of the advantage over the two-handed stroke in the matter of reach. The backswing is usually abbreviated, the arm is held quite stiff, and the racquet is brought forward without the classic initial outward arc. The chances of developing "tennis elbow" are increased because it easily happens that the racquet is pulled into the hit with a leading elbow instead of sent with a momentum-powered swing.

Players seem to adapt very easily to this alternative to the classic swing. The arm is much stronger held close in on the backhand side than in the extended position. There is a sense of security and appropriateness in the direction of motion of the racquet since it travels forward in a path that is almost continuously in the line of the hit. While the stance is usually directly sideways it is not quite as closed as for the classic, so the view of the opposite court can remain relatively good throughout.

THE POSSIBILITIES FOR IMPROVEMENT

When the initially learned techniques happen to be wrong there are many serious obstacles to improvement. Perhaps one of the biggest is the tremendous sense of insecurity that comes with attempts to use any other than an already insecure technique. One of the least recognized of the obstacles is the feeling of deprivation, as has been discussed. Another important source of anxiety on the backhand is the feeling of weakness in the arm in the extended position, especially when accentuated by the use of push.

But with the knowledge of the principles of hitting outlined herein, and through the constant monitoring of the satisfactions obtained with the better methods as well as the unpleasantness associated with the wrong, the choices will become clear and the desired shot, whatever the style, can gradually be perfected.

Notes on

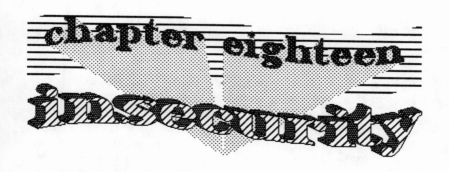

chapter eighteen
insecurity

Stroke production tends to be more attitude and habit limited than task or talent limited. It is a very rare individual who is really incapable of using a rational swing, easily returning a very hard hit ball, getting good pace on a serve, volleying effectively, or doing whatever else a person may assume to be beyond personal capabilities. Many inexpert players can execute nearly any stroke reasonably well in practice. But when the emphasis is on results, especially in a game, the old irrationality takes over.

Mental factors that can unhinge the sanity of a person's game include over aggressive emotions and urges at one extreme, and at the other the equally significant but not as apparent inner feelings of insecurity and insufficiency. When all else is in order these latter anxieties can still forestall any changes for the better. A little discussion of some of the common fears may help players recognize and fight these obstacles to a good game.

SELF DOUBTS

Misgivings about lack of talent develop mostly out of repeated failure to introduce change. There is also apt to be a sense of defeatism stemming from the common notion that nothing can be done about a game that was learned without the right amount and kind of early coaching. The net result is a belief that the existing flaws are permanent and that no new start can be made. These inner fears need to be dealt with before, or at least along with, trying to deal with the defects in the mechanics of the strokes. This is not at all easy because for one thing inner feelings do not have the visibility of physical actions.

Fears not only inhibit attempts at mastering desired stroke patterns but sometimes introduce compensations for problems and limitations that are entirely imaginary and do not exist. An imagined insufficiency generally simulates the very insufficiency feared, and the compensations generated for the imagined are likely to be the same as for the real.

THE LURE OF THE UNATTAINABLE

Paradoxically, fears sometimes develop out of trying for an over-ambitious goal, as when a person has intentions of obtaining a pace that is unattainable in reality with any type of technique. Players having such compulsions soon discover that standard stroke patterns are not capable of producing the fantasy-land results.

The letdown is likely to lead to the adoption of desperation techniques that preclude realization of even ordinary level results. Trying for a little more is often synonymous with playing a little worse. So then there are real problems in addition to the imaginary to contend with, and a sense of athletic inadequacy sets in about being able to hit the ball with any respectable control or pace at all.

LAYERS OF FEARS

An instance of insecurity of a different nature occurs on the serves of some lower level recreational players. Incredible though it seems, there sometimes actually appears to be a fear of not being able to hit the ball over the net. The swing of people with this phobia becomes a desperate shove involving the whole body, something like the action in a shotput.

In most such cases it is not likely that the shove actually originated out of a fear of not being able to hit hard, but rather out of concerns about not being able to control the ball with a full, free swing. The reluctance to swing freely coupled with a desire to use strength to drive the ball over the net with great pace amounts to simultaneous surrender to two incompatible urges, both of which are badly flawed in themselves.

The consequent poor pace obtained with a means as unsuitable as a shove can then get to be interpreted as a personal inadequacy rather than recognized as merely the natural outcome of deficient concepts and techniques. The shove will not be abandoned because it has become habit, and because its use is still motivated by the now enlarged fears concerning control. The embellishments that get added to the stroke in an attempt to regain lost pace do not improve the prospects for obtaining that objective either. Thus new and unnecessary fears are born.

A similar situation exists when a player loses confidence and moves the hitting point more toward the net to take advantage of the fact that the arm is stronger there, and because the eye can follow the ball more easily out in front. This opens up the stance, which in turn limits the forward travel of the racquet, narrows the hitting zone, and complicates the timing. Embellishments keep getting added to alleviate the original and the added problems. Valid techniques are replaced with expedients, and the game is on its way to falling apart.

FEAR OF A FAST BALL

A fast approaching ball often raises an instinctive fear in the receiver that the momentum of the ball is much greater than can be handled in a normal manner. Past experiences of shocks to the arm when unsuitable means were used to return very hard hit balls, or when the timing was not adjusted for the extra speed, create defensive attitudes. So when a fast ball comes along the player reacts as if it were necessary to brace for the impact of a heavy object travelling at high speed.

Very few people consciously think that way but very many nevertheless act that way. The body flinches backward, the arm is frozen close in, the eyes may be shut protectively tight, and a quick, short turn of the body is substituted for a normal swing. The reaction is as if it were first necessary to expend a great amount of effort merely to stop the ball and then to expend all the additional effort that by itself would produce the outgoing pace.

If this notion were correct the receiver would have to use more than double the effort expended by the opponent on any shot: one measure to absorb the momentum of the oncoming ball, one to provide an at least equal outgoing pace, and something extra to make up for losses and top the incoming pace. A feeling of insufficiency for such a task would be very well founded since such abnormal demands on a person's strength and energy would make any hard hit ball practically unreturnable.

REUSE THE MOMENTUM

But the above described notion is entirely irrational, as is obvious in the light of the earlier discussions on elasticity. The momentum of the oncoming ball is not destroyed but is first stored in the elasticities and then, with proper technique, reconverted into pace. The advantage for the receiver is that the pace is already there. It is wrong to try to add much more. The greater the oncoming pace the less effort, not more, needed for a maximum paced return.

In case the formula for the development of pace given in the chapter on "ELASTICITY" has been forgotten it is "ball velocity plus twice racquet velocity." Some readers may find it advantageous to review that chapter at this time since the mere knowledge of the theoretical formula, out of the context of the discussion about its limitations in the world of reality, is likely to cause the formula to be misapplied.

Racquet velocity has to be optimized not maximized. If, for instance, a serve is approaching at 110 miles per hour (110 mph) it is not practical to expect the return to travel even faster. In order to define the amount of energy that can be expended usefully in this case it is necessary to make two initial assumptions for use in a few simple calculations. One assumption is that a very good speed can be achieved on the ground stroke return, say 90 mph. Another is that a high level of efficiency can be attained in the recovery of energy from the elasticities, say 60 percent.

Under the given conditions the recovered ball velocity amounts to 66 mph (110 × .60). The difference between this and the desired 90 mph is 24 mph. This has to come from two sources: 100 percent of the racquet "carrying" velocity plus 60 percent of that part of

187

the stored energy that is derived from racquet momentum (not ball momentum). So the 24 mph is equivalent to 160 percent of racquet velocity. Dividing 24 mph by 1.60 gives 15 mph for the necessary racquet velocity.

Using a similar set of calculations for a ball approaching at 80 mph it will be found that to attain a return speed of 90 mph the racquet velocity has to be 26.25 mph, still a modest figure. Greater racquet velocities will increase ball velocity, but the law of diminishing returns sets in sooner or later depending on the skills of the player and the properties of the equipment. Another problem is that when a person wants to hit very hard it often happens that the quality of execution deteriorates, the error rate rises, conversion efficiency gets to be very poor, and the ball speed is quite often lowered instead of raised.

As can be readily deduced from the above figures, very high racquet speeds would in theory create ball velocities that are not realistically attainable. In the example of a ball approaching at a good speed of 80 mph, for instance, if the racquet speed is raised to 60 mph the return ball speed, even with only 60 percent efficiency, would be 144 mph. This is far past what can be reasonably expected. Yet most mediocre players in such situations are more likely to try to swing at 60 mph or more for a ball speed that is not attainable, than to swing at 26.25 mph for a really fine and yet realizable ball velocity of 90 mph.

The main intents in returning a fast ball should be to prepare early and execute calmly, bearing in mind that it is not appropriate to try to supply much new energy. The ball can be hit a very trifle ahead of the normal hitting point to take advantage of the fact that the eye can follow the ball better there, and because when the arm is out in front it is effectively braced to both counter the heavy impact and reuse the existing pace. That should be the major intent: reuse the existing pace.

The thing not to do is to assume that it is necessary to use every bit of strength and energy or that otherwise the return pace will be less than the received, and that a concession of inferiority will be made thereby causing the loss of both status and the match. It invites disaster to either resort to compulsive exertions or to freeze in sheer fright. Extra fast balls should not be considered to pose a difficulty as much as presenting a challenge and an opportunity.

EXPLOITING THE MISUSE OF EFFORT

An advantage that the receiver may be able to exploit is that the opponent may be off balance after using maximum effort for a very hard hit, and may be having more than normal difficulty in getting into position and being ready for the return. When a player hits extra hard the time available to get back into the ready position will be somewhat shorter than normal. Any fairly solid return may therefore catch him unready and off balance. But it is not something that can always be depended on because an alternative effect could be a more aggressive attitude and a more alert court coverage.

GETTING CAUTIOUS

Another genre of insecurity is evidenced in the miniature swings so commonly used by recreational players. Long, free strokes are synonymous with mastery and confidence, items in short supply wherever there are or have been problems with technique. Even expert players often suffer the effects of feelings of insecurity. They may then, like their inferiors, easily abandon the easy and natural way of doing things to resort to caution and compromise. Rather than that the errors will be reduced thereby there will likely be a multiplication. Caution in the swing, being an emotionally induced variation from the norm, will introduce errors in timing just as surely as will one that is overly aggressive.

Even after a player has partially mastered an improved stroke and the time comes to use it in a game the feelings of insecurity associated with unfamiliar new methods, and a fear of making errors, usually cause quick reversion to the old habits. This is a serious predicament since those techniques that a player relies on in the more important circumstances will inevitably get to be used all the time. Not only are errors likely to multiply because of the reversion, but the repetition rates are likely to guarantee retention of the bad habits, both old and new.

Of course there are apt to be problems with adopting new techniques, but no more so than with using the inadequate old. The possibility of "might not work" if done the new way is still a much better option than "will not work" if done the old. Hitting does not consist of merely trying to avoid problems.

Quite a few players fully intend to use only smooth, expert level strokes ultimately, but they nevertheless stick with the old faults during play with the reservation that these are temporary expedients to be used until the better techniques are adequately mastered. As pointed out in an earlier chapter this could mean that the old habits are being practiced several hundred times as much as the probably never to be adopted replacements. The logic parallels that of the old saying about not being willing to go into the water until having learned how to swim.

DEPENDENCE ON THE IRRATIONAL

While the inner self can act with a high degree of practical wisdom that hidden side can also operate in a most irrational and unreasoning fashion. The conscious mind could be very rational about wanting to eliminate a mannerism or adopt an obviously better technique, but the subconscious may have reservations and may automatically force the arm to stay with what is familiar. An automatic response just happens, and so is not influenced by conscious decision.

The inner feelings may be equivalent to the following line of reasoning: "I tried to do exactly what the coach told me, but it didn't feel right, and it still is not working the way it should, or as it does for other people. I can't use the coach's corrections because there is something different about me. There is no use taking chances with a swing that I know won't work for me." The above is just one possible way of thinking, and it is not being presented as a standard explanation for the many strange flourishes that players invent and get addicted to with very great ease.

CHANGES FOR THE WORSE

There is an element of danger in assuming that a presumably better new technique should be used regardless of how unpleasant the feel. Some of the unpleasantness will merely be due to unfamiliarity and incomplete mastery, and will have to be tolerated for a while. But some could be due to the new methods being actually technically inferior to the old.

Any ideas that can be related to the principles of elasticity can ordinarily be trusted, and when confirmed by the appreciations derived from the experience of good hits should be the controlling influences in the adoption of new techniques. In this way the new methods, if they are really better, will come to be used because they get to be desired, while the old get to be rejected because they have come to feel decidedly inferior and unpleasant.

The three main choices available to the student in dealing with inner fears regarding the use of new methods are: (1) reversion to the old habits (which usually happens), (2) just trying to establish familiarity with the new via a great deal of practice of patterns (which probably won't do much good), or (3) becoming familiar with the principles of hitting and learning to appreciate the feel and the techniques of a really smooth hit, and thereby becoming dissatisfied with the old eccentricities.

Ignoring fears and just imitating patterns does not address the mental side of the problem. Fears will not be made to disappear by paying no attention to them. Wherever a fear is either evident or suspected the coach can devise drills that are not very demanding on the student but yet will demonstrate that the ideas of insufficiency are nothing more than hobgoblins. In general the approach is to show that what the student may consider to be too difficult is actually very easy: returning a hard hit ball, or getting pace with an easy swing, for instance.

A bonus from an understanding of the physical principles behind a good hit and an appreciation of the feel will be a growing confidence that the ideal techniques will work just as well for oneself as for anybody else.

Discovering that fact and developing that confidence will go a long way toward overcoming the influence of fears.

PLAY THE BALL

A player's game may fall apart when facing someone who is a level or so higher. Easy shots are flubbed, and the match just becomes an exercise in losing as quickly as possible. But a ball is a ball is a ball. It has to be respected for its own sake and not in relation to the source, which is a court's length remote and without any presence or influence on the receiver's side.

Therefore a given speed and bounce has to get the same respect and attention whether hit by a dub or a pro. Conversely, a given pace and bounce should present no more difficulty if from a pro than if from a dub. The most common mistake is in trying to do too much if from a pro. Granted that the return to the pro may have to be somewhat better than ordinary, but that does not justify trying to hit impossible winners, and on every ball. In any case the player on the other side, if much better, will probably not have much difficulty handling the best shots coming that way.

Trying to hit shots beyond one's capabilities to an opponent who nevertheless will be able to return the best of them usually equates to making a variety of errors off all kinds of easy bounces. To make matters worse, lesser players are generally overdoing their shots to begin with, so trying to do even more merely aggravates a principal existing problem.

Blasting in an attempt to force a weak return may be worth the chance at times, but hitting for better than attainable velocity will never work. Although moderately paced returns may not do much more than go in, making it possible for a superior opponent to take charge and win points easily, that is still much more respectable than giving points away voluntarily via unnecessary errors.

Recourse in game situations to special techniques intended to provide better results than are normally obtainable amounts to voluntary abandonment of what works, even if only after a fashion, in favor of expedients that never work in any situation but merely satisfy the urge to make a violent effort. Putting something extra into a shot should involve increasing the attention and energy allotted to the preparation stage. The usual tendency is to spend even less than the normal amount of those two elements on the preparation and more energy than is available or can be controlled on the forward swing.

There are mental factors that relate less to techniques than to attitudes and psychology, such as the fear of losing to a lesser player, the reluctance to appear to try when playing against or with someone considered to be of lower rank, the loss of all interest and incentive over a bad line call, etc. It can merely be noted here again that a ball is a ball is a ball. Emotions have no influence on the ball, but they can interfere with execution.

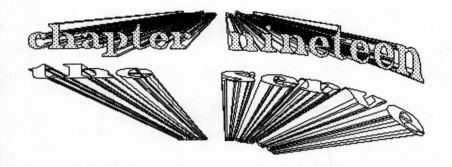

The serves of most recreational players cannot honestly be described as anything better than awful. The first serve is the one stroke where most players always hit as violently as possible in spite of getting error rates of seventy percent or more, sometimes even at the expert level. The problems inherent in a serve include exceptional complexity, resistance to improvement, and vulnerability to emotional execution. The difficulties provide a good test of the efficacy of some of the means that have been suggested here for the upgrading of established games.

THE EFFICIENCY OF THE SWING

It would be difficult to justify the classic service motion on the basis of efficiency and conservation of energy. While there can be some retention of momentum there is bound to be considerable loss, mostly in three up or down reversals of direction: (1) the racquet drops down toward the ground, (2) reverses upward to a position above the head, (3) reverses down behind the back to below shoulder level, (4) reverses upward and accelerates as it goes high over the head, and (5) turns forward and continues to accelerate as it meets the ball.

THE EFFICIENCY OF THE WINDUP

On the classic serve many players slow the racquet motion near the peak of the first upward move to the extent of almost or even actually coming to a dead stop. When this occurs all the prior motion of the arm merely operates to put the arm and the racquet into whatever form of last stage ready position the individual uses before the final accelerating and hitting loop of the swing.

If a person who is in the habit of having the racquet come to such a stop can place the racquet and the body into the same ready position without the help of the previous motions, and can toss the ball easily and effectively from that posture, then there is little or no physical advantage to the customary prior activities.

But getting the whole body prepared and ready to contribute to the hitting action is not an insignificant achievement. Even the baseball pitcher, whose motions are not complicated by the presence of a racquet, will typically go through a surprisingly elaborate and individualistic windup preparatory to the act of moving the arm through the final arc of the throw. While servers are entitled to equivalent preliminaries, the windups of some inexpert players go past all reason with spectacular and extensive rituals involving many extraneous motions and a sizable expenditure of energy.

Some players introduce a halt in the motion of the body also. Of those who do not only a small percent manage the timing of body motion well enough to derive anywhere near the available benefit in the form of added racquet momentum and reinforcement of the arm with the body. At the instant of the hit the big majority of players have already taken the body well past the point where it ought to be even at that late stage.

THE BIG CIRCLE

On the serve, if anyplace, the racquet travels in something of a circle just before the hit. Since the circumference of a circle is over six times the length of its radius, the advantages obtained by extending the arm and using wrist and arm flex to maximize the momentum of the racquet and the resultant pace of the ball can be readily understood. A smaller than maximum circle is not an unmitigated evil however, because the arm is stronger close in and will provide good racquet acceleration if the motion remains a swing.

However the use of a small circle is generally due to a sense of insecurity about the weakness of the arm and about getting the ball to land in court. Players at all levels of skill develop difficulties in their service motion because of a common tendency to bring the elbow in and push at the ball at critical times. There is a feeling of security and control in pushing the racquet in the intended direction of the hit even though that confidence is highly unjustified. The hitting motion may then be directed downward, the ball hit from a lower than desirable height, the racquet velocity decreased, and the probability of error increased. In fact, just in the past year the use of push caused double fault on match point in several "grand slam" finals.

The worry about accuracy is often compounded by a desire to use an extravagant amount of strength. These urges are apt to result in an action that is a combination of a muscular shove and a downward pull. The pull is intended to somehow influence the ball to change its path and curve downward when it reaches the net. The racquet velocity is diminished by the shove, as well as by the laid back wrist that is the natural accompaniment, and diverted into other than the desired line of travel by the pull.

Extending the racquet arm to near maximum and trying not to tense the shoulder muscles will help minimize the tendency to push rather than swing the racquet. An extra benefit from an extended arm is an enlargement of the area in the service box into which the ball can be directed. A considerably more extensive discussion of this effect, and the general problem of hitting the target area, is presented later on in this chapter.

COMPARISON TO A THROW

The classic service motion has frequently been likened to a throw. While there is considerable similarity between the two, the serve is different from at least some throwing patterns in that for most serves a near full upward extension of the arm is used. In many throwing motions the hand travels forward at only about head height, which puts the arm at considerably less than full extension. A tall person with a strong arm may be able to hit excellent serves in spite of a low toss and a throw-like swing, but for others the results are generally less than good.

One feature of the throw that deserves to be emulated, not only in serves but in most ground strokes, is that the arm is accelerated forward in the direction of the throw as the ball leaves the hand. Many servers hit only a glancing blow by curtailing the forward travel of the racquet and bringing it downward in a circle at the hit.

The concept of throwing can be useful for another reason. In throwing a ball at a target there is automatic allowance for the effects of gravity. By contrast, the common mistake in a serve is to ignore the effects of gravity and think in terms of hitting the ball along a downward sloped straight line pointing directly at a spot in the service court. The falsity of that notion will be demonstrated further on in this chapter.

THE PRINCIPLES OF THE HIT

The essential fact of a serve is that it is a hit. As such, the factors of elasticity, restoring forces, appropriate grip and body position, use of the momentum in a swing rather than the strength in a push, accelerating the racquet through contact, extending the arm to optimize the length of the arc, straightening the arc out in the direction of the hit during contact (except for special effects), using wrist and arm flex, moving the body into the hit, reinforcing the arm with the body, rotating the shoulder into the hit, avoiding rotating the shoulder or the body ahead of the hit, optimizing the hitting point, etc., must all get their due respect, but in the context of a hit and not as individual details. How could it be possible to direct the attention to several of them simultaneously? And what would the consequences be of watching only one?

The general requirements for the hitting point are the same as for other strokes: where the combination of good direction, momentum, and attitude of racquet, strength and freedom of the arm and wrist, reinforcement with the body, and availability of body motion and rotation into the swing are as close to optimum as possible. More descriptively it can simply be said that the hit should occur at the good part of the swing.

One of the factors that makes the serve different from most other shots is that the ball has zero initial velocity. Although this means that there is no initial momentum of the ball to be overcome it also means that there is none to add to the energies stored and recovered via the elasticities. So all the forward pace of the ball must be obtained from energy generated in the swing of the racquet.

Consequently a non-rigid grip and a great deal of wrist and arm flex are not only permissible but desirable in most serves as a means of increasing the amount of momentum that can be developed in the racquet. By those means the serve generates the fastest pace in tennis, in spite of the zero initial ball velocity.

THE DIFFICULTY OF A SIMPLE TOSS

Besides the satisfactory accomplishment of the details that pertain to the optimizing of the swing there is another very important element to master in a serve: a proper toss. It is surely a highly emphasized point in just about every coach's teaching routine, and is a simple enough skill to master in itself. Among good players there is a great deal of similarity in the toss. But among others there is an incredible variety of inappropriate means of placing the ball with great inconsistency into positions from which it can be hit only with difficulty, and with undependable aim and insignificant pace.

The toss presents no problem to those people who learned it correctly initially. But, for reasons to be explained, it is a most formidable obstacle to those who did not. Practising the toss is very tedious because it is easily possible to do fifteen or more in the space of only one minute. So it is a rare individual who is determined enough to practice it for more than several minutes on more than several occasions. Such a minuscule amount of repetition will not produce improvement in spite of the simplicity of the basic skill.

COMPATIBILITY WITH THE SWING

Even if perfection is achieved in the toss itself there is then a new problem in that there is a lack of compatibility with the existing imperfect service motion, which latter may bring the racquet around with inappropriate timing in a path that never comes close to the correct hitting point. A player with a peculiar or erratic service motion has to modify the toss correspondingly, and is forced to do for the bad swing what a previously cited adage instructs one to do for the good: "toss at the swing." This has to mean goodbye perfect toss.

The "toss at the swing" idea is valid only in the context of using an ideal swing. So the maxim is somewhat redundant since by that definition a good toss is not a variable at all. The advice might be more applicable if it said "toss to where the swing ought to go." A way to start to implement that concept is to intend to use a visualized ideal swing and to toss in the plane of that swing. In other words, the stroke is first visualized and then acted out.

With the path of the racquet thus established all that remains is to get the ball to the preordained hitting point when the racquet inevitably arrives there. If the server has a firm purpose to go through with the complete stroke in that manner, without any accommodations for a misplaced toss or concessions to feelings of insecurity, then there will be a gradual improvement in consistency in placing the ball at the appropriate hitting point at the right time.

Since the swing should not be modified to meet a misplaced toss there should be little or no attention paid to the details of the toss while it is being made. A bad toss will only get worse with increased observation, while at the same time the swing will fall apart from neglect. If the ball does not get to the desired location then it is time to reflect postmortem on the controlling inner motives or other factors that directed the toss elsewhere.

PRACTICING THE TOSS

There is an occasionally used drill involving a sequence of three tosses that can both increase the amount of practice of the toss that a player is willing to make and facilitate the coordination of the toss with the swing. The exercise refines the concept of where the hitting point should be and establishes the processes by which the toss is matched to an ideal swing.

First two practice tosses are made combined with the swing, but with the swing stopped just before the final forward motion into the hit. The swing should be completely real in all other respects, including the requirement that the body fully express all the intents associated with a satisfying hit. Otherwise the exercise merely amounts to practicing improper readiness and a toss adapted for that condition.

When practicing tosses without going through with the actual hit that final action must always be visualized so that the intents as to a smooth, relaxed swing get to be reconciled with the location of the toss, and vice versa. This is where the slow motion type of visualization process, SMV, can help bridge the gap between idea and reality.

When learning the toss it is advisable to also learn to vary the placement and height slightly. The objectives include to remain flexible, test the advantages of various hitting points, remove any restrictions on the placement of the toss and on the nature of progressive improvements to the swing pattern, and allow for possible changes in placement for use with different serves. The shifts should be small and the toss made as nearly the same as possible for all serves for reasons of disguise.

COMBINING TOSS AND SWING

On the third toss of the sequence of three a moderately paced swing can be carried all the way through in the manner visualized, but only if the toss is reasonably like what is understood to be ideal. Initially it seldom will be. The swing should not be permitted to go wild, but kept both real and ideal.

The swing is a big problem in itself, and an immense problem in combination with the rather simple toss. A person can very easily acquire a good mastery of tossing to an ideal hitting point, but unless the swing is perfected enough to have the racquet pass through that hitting point there will be an automatic refusal to use an ideal toss. The body is smart enough not to direct the ball and the racquet to different hitting points. The bad toss and bad swing at least work together. So initially the first two tosses will tend to be fine while the third will almost inevitably go out of control.

A concept that may be used to help stabilize the toss is to think of having the arm follow the ball upwards, since a common flaw is to flip the ball up instead of more like lifting it up. But the concepts of the swing should control the toss, not the other way around. Concentration on the swing can be practiced by adding an initial "toss" to the sequence of three, this time using an imaginary ball together with a complete but moderate swing containing no omissions, exaggerations, or excesses.

When practicing ground strokes it is not possible to entirely avoid chasing the ball with the racquet, especially in the case of unpredictable behavior by the ball. But on practice serves there should be very few such compromises. If the racquet approaches the ideal hitting point and the ball is not going to be there the swing should not be changed to chase the errant ball. Otherwise the good habits fail to get mastered, the old are practiced and perpetuated, and new bad habits are formed.

Even if the ball is missed completely it is still a useful drill if a proper swing is used. But a swing compromised to fit a bad toss, or vice versa, means that both are being practiced in a wrong way. Once the body finds out that the toss will be compromised it will always intend to use the old swing.

A practice serve should not be completed if there is a chance of a mis-hit causing too great of a shock to the arm, or any possibility at all that somebody else could be endangered by a badly misdirected ball. A good place for initial drills is against a tall backboard or wall, and with no windows or people in the way.

The toss and the swing must be used at all times as described above, both in practice and as much as possible in play. When in play, though, there ordinarily should not be any practice tosses. But there should be the same intent for an ideal swing as described above, not reversion to something considered to be more suited to the practicalities involved with winning a point. It is unwise to abandon what is effective in practice for what has been proven to be unsatisfactory in play.

As the sequence of three or four tosses of the drill is repeated there should be an attempt to improve on all the concepts involved, but in a general way, not individually: stance, grip, preparation, readiness, toss, swing, shoulder turn, acceleration, hitting point, end position of racquet, etc. After both the toss and the swing get to be reasonably well mastered only the full serve need be practiced.

It is necessary to be on the lookout for compromises, compensations, muscling, body ahead of arm, emotional execution, etc. Extensive use of SMV is advisable. Only the elements of the swing and toss should be pictured when using visualizations, not the behavior of the ball after the hit. Placing the emphasis on results neglects the matters that produce the results.

The drills described above mitigate the problem of which should be learned first, the toss or the swing, since both are learned together. Even a novice, who has not yet developed a serve and has no bad habits to forget, will have trouble retaining a pattern for the toss when it is to be combined with the swing if the toss was learned by itself first.

THE TIMING OF THE TOSS

There is an adage that on the toss the racquet arm and the tossing arm should go up together. Would that anything in tennis was that simple. The statement is only partially true, and so can be a source of trouble if taken literally. The technique of having the arms go up approximately together is a good way for beginners to learn the elements of the toss, but it may mean nothing but trouble for people whose perfectly good manner of tossing does not fit that pattern exactly. Observation of the experts shows that there is much subtle variation.

If two people of the same build toss to slightly different heights it is obvious that if in each case the two arms start together then the accommodation for the variation in the height has to be made someplace else in one of the swings. Either that or one of the players has to start the ball arm sooner or later than the other, else the ball will not be at the hitting point when the racquet gets there. Additional sources of variation include a pause at the peak of the first upward move of the racquet, a jump during the swing, and differences in the extension of the arm and the velocities of the swings.

So if the adage is believed it could cause some people to try to do something other than what they normally do when serving confidently and well. Even top players with very good serves can be misled. When trouble is being experienced with the serve they may attempt to settle down by trying to bring both arms up together. Sometimes they will even practice the motions just before a serve. If this is not the exact norm, and it seldom is exactly so, the troubles can only get worse.

THE WINDMILL SERVE

There are a very few people who use a circular windmill type swing. Examples of this serve can occasionally be seen even in top tournaments, although sometimes only because the user has a shoulder injury that is aggravated by the use of the conventional motion. The technique is uncommon enough that many players are not even aware of its existence.

The racquet is simply taken down, back, up, and forward in a largely circular path with no interruptions or reversals of racquet direction. The elbow remains relatively unbent throughout, although a little wrist and arm flex can be used.

There is quite a bit of racquet velocity built up since it is developed gradually and continuously without any reversals. By contrast, in the conventional swing a good part of the racquet velocity begins to be developed only after the racquet has reached the "back scratch" position, placing a large and sudden strain on the muscles of the arm and shoulder at that time. The windmill serve properly done should impose less of a strain on those muscles and on the tendons in the elbow.

The arm is easily and naturally kept at full extension with the method, so the hit generally occurs at a commendable height. All in all, there seems to be no reason why the ball cannot be hit harder with the windmill serve than with the classic swing. However to accomplish that type of result the body must get involved, not just stay rigid and uncooperative while the arm travels the almost circular path on its own.

PRINCIPLES vs. PATTERNS

There is no single best serve for all people. This is by no means intended to denigrate the classic, which is really great, but to emphasize the necessity of basing the serve on the mechanics of hitting. If a pattern is economical in terms of the energy required and also produces a good hit then it is fine and appropriate.

Correctly executed, but without some of the petty restrictions such as using a specific alignment of the feet or having the racquet come to a stop in a certain position, the genuine classic serve is synonymous with correct mechanics. Some patterns that are decidedly unclassical nevertheless incorporate the correct mechanics equally effectively.

An important advantage of using the basic requirements of a hit rather than a pattern as the guide is that as the concepts of the service hit are refined, or of any stroke, all others will share in the benefits, and all can be further improved on without any defined limit. When ideas are open to continual expansion and improvement then what feels correct today may subsequently in the light of further experience and knowledge feel quite abbreviated and inadequate. The desired game is something like the horizon, forever receding even though where it appeared to be previously may have been reached and even exceeded.

If the approach used is the emulation of a pattern then that pattern represents the upper limit of achievement. Even when it gets to be mastered it may turn out to be wrong in some respect, or unsuitable, or just below what is attainable through a more complete mastery of the art of hitting. If the hit is not as good as it can be there is something about the pattern or the mechanics of the hit that is not right, whether there is ostensible conformance to some established style or not. There is no such thing as having done everything absolutely right and yet not having obtained a correspondingly superior result.

THE HITTING POINT

The analyses under this and the following five subheadings into the nature of common sources of error are based on the classic serve or close variants, but the comments are nevertheless quite general in nature and apply to most other patterns as well.

The hitting point on a serve should be slightly forward of the body because the reinforcement is better and the arm is stronger out front. However if the hitting point is too far forward then various problems arise, such as cutting down on the remaining available racquet travel, slowing down of the racquet before contact, lowering of the hitting point, and angling the face of the racquet both more downward and toward the side.

A consequent problem is that as the body (or perhaps the subconscious) becomes aware of the incorrect direction and the unpleasant feel it introduces compensations. These soon become habit. For instance, if by the time of contact the natural angle of the face of the racquet would direct the ball too much toward the ground the player will learn to compensate by laying the wrist back to bring the angle up to normal. While helping the aim this will introduce other new problems.

THE FACE-THE-NET COMPULSION

One of the most universal of faults in serves is the breaking of the reinforcement with the body. In a serve this can occur in two directions: horizontally and vertically. In the horizontal type the body is rotated around too soon, similar to the same problem in ground strokes. When the body gets ahead in that way it leaves the arm in a weak position for the forward swing.

A very common form of this fault is to go through the windup in a more or less exemplary sideways position, but then swivel the body around prematurely, or just the torso. This moves at least the upper part of the body into a face-the-net position before the arm has made comparable progress in the forward swing. The usual main psychological urges behind the premature turn of the body are to use the strength of the entire physique to the utmost and to look at the point where the ball is intended to land. The turn at the hit should be for the purpose of augmenting and completing the hit, not watching the progress of the ball.

The intent to maximize the use of strength neglects the fact that the body is disproportionately stronger than the arm and must be restrained from either going all out or acting too soon. The arm should be able to push off against the shoulder and not be dragged along by it. Some body rotation should be used, but only in a manner to have the shoulder send the arm into the hit to give added force and power. A too early body turn will waste this extra power and leave the arm behind fighting to catch up.

In some such faulty serves the premature rotation is quite subtle, with the swivel of the body only partially preceding the swing. In these cases the player may find it difficult to believe that the turn of the body nevertheless occurred somewhat before the hit, and that both the forward swing and hit occurred in an essentially face-the-net position.

The turn to face the net is very predominant in recreational level senior players. Here it is often due to feelings of insecurity about being able to aim accurately at a spot not in the line of vision with the toss. Facing the net, or just opening the stance too soon, also originates out of a desire to rely on strength for speed and a push for accuracy. Strength is not a factor in abundant supply among seniors, and the push is a technique with the least rewards in terms of pace and the greatest penalties in terms of strain. In its extreme the total action may begin to resemble a throw executed with the wrong foot forward.

THE FORWARD JACKKNIFE

Breaking reinforcement vertically simply means bending the body forward in a jackknife action. The arm cannot bring the racquet along as quickly as the body is capable of folding itself forward and downward. So although the arm continues in the forward direction it lags further and further back with respect to the body. The racquet is then dragged downward rather than swung forward into the hit.

A common instruction intended to keep the head up and prevent the forward jackknife is to hold the tossing arm up in the extended position as long as possible. This does have some effectiveness even though it amounts to controlling the body position by means of a detail. There is also at least some penalty in terms of interference with the swing. A better way is to continually refine the concept of the hit so that eventually the feel of the downward bend of the body, and of the racquet arm being left behind, will get to be considered unpleasant.

Another means of controlling the tendency to jackknife is to intend to accelerate the racquet into the top of the swing, not all the way into the bottom. This counteracts the jackknife since a corollary of the latter is an acceleration on the way down, which is well after the ball has left the racquet. A good concept of the hit will both improve the hit and correct the jackknife, while just working on the flaw alone is not likely to bring about significant improvement in either.

211

Both the horizontal and the vertical means of breaking reinforcement overwhelm the strength of the arm. When that happens the jolt of the impact created by the inertia of the stationary ball will deflect the racquet head backward with respect to the arm. With that relationship changed the attitude of the racquet at the hit is unpredictable, and so is the direction of the ball.

AUXILIARY ACTIONS

In tennis there often are actions that involve trade-offs between several desired objectives. Jumping into the air is one such action. Jumping on the serve extends the reach, enlarges the target area, can provide a quick start for an advance to the net, and can be an outlet for the urge to use every last bit of effort. But keeping at least one foot in firm contact with the ground tends to improve the reinforcement, increase ball velocity, improve control, and economize on effort.

One type of motion that is fairly common but provides no discernible benefit or trade-off is to let the body drift sideways during the swing. The racquet is pulled away from the hit, decreasing both pace and accuracy.

SCIENCE OF HITTING THE TARGET AREA

Hitting to a selected point in the service court is the source of an amazing amount of difficulty and misunderstanding. Many people never realize that a straight line extended in the initial direction of the ball should point to an area well past where the ball is intended to land, and that it is incredibly bad science on the serve to aim directly at some point in the service box.

They incorrectly assume that a racquet held over the head has an unobstructed view of most or at least a sizable part of the service court. They also very incorrectly assume that the trajectory of a hard hit ball is a straight line.

THE STRAIGHT LINE FACTS

The figures below apply to the condition that the real or the straight line trajectories represent the path of the bottom of the ball, from the hit to the ground.

A little geometry will show that a straight line drawn from a quite high hitting point of 8½ feet above the baseline, and angled down to just clear the 3 foot high point of the net, will touch ground 3.3 inches past the service line. If the straight line is raised just one inch at the location of the net then the point where it touches ground will be 14.4 inches outside the service court. So in this case one inch at the net multiplies the error at the service line by more than four. Fortunately the ball does not travel in a straight line, even with no topspin.

A line drawn similarly from a more common height of 8 feet will touch ground about 2 feet 5 inches past the service line. This can be confirmed without mathematics by simply climbing a stepladder at the baseline until the eye is 8 feet above the ground. A little experimentation will show that the eye has to be at a height of 8 feet 7 inches before the edge of the service line becomes visible above the 3 foot high point of the net. Those readers who are mathematically inclined can confirm the given figures with a simple application of the proportions of similar triangles.

THE IDEA OF THE TRAJECTORY

It is very difficult for the server to be aware of the exact initial direction of the ball. The attitude of the racquet changes constantly during the serve, the racquet is faced downward right after the hit, and the ball eventually travels down into the court. These events tend to create the illusion that the ball was hit downward even though the initial direction was actually more horizontal, or may even have been upward.

It is obvious that if a ball travelling in the initial direction in a straight line will just clear the net then the least downward pull of gravity will send the ball into the net, and there is plenty of downward pull and motion due to gravity as will be shown. At the instant that a ball is departing from the racquet the initial straight line heading should pass well above the net and should be directed at a spot well beyond the service line, not, as is commonly attempted, barely above the net, or even a little below so as to be aimed directly at a spot inside the service court.

When the ball is made to just barely skim over the net it will normally land in court by several feet, which is too far in. However for many good servers the allowance for the trajectory is more on the basis of experience than accurate observation. For them aiming just above the net is effectively equivalent to actually aiming so that the initial heading and the effects of gravity combine to produce the necessary clearance at the net.

A temporary expedient that may help with the aim is to visualize the curved path of the ball as being displayed by a thin streak of light or color. The server should think of hitting out in the initial direction of that streak, not at the end point or at any location along the way. The path can also be visualized as being a string, or a tube, or whatever other device fits in with a person's way of thinking.

With the direction of the ball thus pre-established there is then less temptation to divert attention from the hit to watching the flight of the ball, and less tendency to turn the body too quickly to be able to do that watching better. The concept can be useful with other types of strokes also. However the idea is being advanced mainly as a means to help clear up misconceptions and to assist in the development of a proper set of intents, not to suggest that observation of a detail during normal stroke production is desirable.

THE SCIENCE OF THE TRAJECTORY

Be assured that the path of a serve is not a straight line. It may look straight in the case of serves hit with a good deal of pace, but it is not. Although the cumulative drop by the time the ball reaches the net is not small it may be practically imperceptible because it is occurring all along the path of travel.

For instance, neglecting the effects of spin and air friction, it can be shown that a ball hit with a blazing horizontal speed of 110 miles per hour (110 mph) will have a drop due to gravity of a little over 11 inches by the time it traverses the 39 feet to the net. And the drop will increase to a total of more than 2 feet 2 inches by the time the ball covers the additional 21 feet to the service line.

With a more realistic but still very respectable horizontal speed of 80 mph, the drop due to gravity will be over 1 foot 9 inches at the net and over 4 feet 2 inches by the time the ball gets to the service line. This means that a ball hit at a very decent speed of 80 mph must leave the racquet as if headed for a point almost 2 feet above the top of the net in order for the ball to just clear the net. And if the hit is made at a height of 7 feet the ball will land about 3 feet 2 inches inside the service line, which at expert level tennis is too far in.

Neglecting the effects of spin and air friction again, if the ball is hit at about 47.5 mph from a height of 8 feet, or at about 53 mph from a height of 7 feet, the ball will have to be aimed straight out initially to just clear the 3 foot high point of the net. Below those speeds at those heights the ball will actually have to be directed upward to just get over the net.

The following table gives various data in feet and inches for both the "real" and "straight line" trajectories of serves hit at various speeds. The trajectories labeled "real" are so only in the sense of taking gravity into account, but not spin and air friction. The "straight line" trajectories are extended from the initial heading of the ball when leaving the racquet. The up-

	110 MPH	80 MPH	53 MPH	47.5 MPH	H
GRVT AT	2' 2.6"	4' 2.2"	9' 6.4"	11' 10.4"	7
S LINE	2' 2.6"	4' 2.2"	9' 6.4"	11' 10.4"	8
RL PT	− 0.6"	0' 4.8"	1' 7.4"	2' 1.8"	7
ABOVE NT	0' 3.6"	0' 9.0"	1' 11.6"	2' 6.0"	8
ST LN	0' 10.7"	2' 2.0"	5' 7.8"	7' 2.0"	7
ABOVE NT	1' 2.9"	2' 6.2"	6' 0 "	7' 6.2"	8
ST LN	27' 9.0"	89' 2.0"	——	——	7
OUT	22' 11.0"	65' 9.0"	——	——	8
SKIM NT	− 5.5"	3' 2.4"	8' 5.4"	9' 9.7"	7
IN CRT	2' 7.9"	5' 4.2"	9' 6.5"	10' 8.2"	8

per line of each pair relates to balls hit from a height of 7 feet, while the lower line of each pair relates to balls hit from a height of 8 feet, as indicated in the column titled "H."

The column headings in the top line of the table give the speed of the ball in miles per hour. The next four pairs of lines ("GRVT AT S LINE," "RL PT ABOVE NT," "ST LN ABOVE NT," and "ST LN OUT") contain data associated with balls that land right on the service line. The last pair of lines (SKIM NT IN CRT) give the landing points of balls that just clear the net in "real" trajectories.

Each dimension in the pair of lines titled "GRVT AT S LINE" (for "gravitational drop at service line") gives the total cumulative drop due to gravity by the time the ball gets to and lands right on the service line. Since this particular drop depends solely on the time it takes for the ball to travel the distance to the service line the figures are the same whether the ball is hit from a height of seven feet or eight feet.

The figures in the pair of lines titled "RL PT ABOVE NT" (for "real point above net") give the clearances by which the ball would pass over the net in the "real" trajectories. Three feet have to be added to the given clearances to get the height of the ball above the ground.

The figures in the pair of lines titled "ST LN ABOVE NT" (for "straight line above net") give the clearances by which the ball would pass over the net if it actually travelled a straight line along the initial direction. As with "RL PT ABOVE NT," three feet have to be added to get the height of the ball above the ground. Doing this for the figures given for 53 and 47.5 mph shows that the initial direction has to be upward for the ball to land on the service line.

The figures in the pair of lines titled "ST LN OUT" (for "straight line out") give the distances past the service line, instead of on it, where the ball would land if it actually travelled in the mentioned straight lines. There is no such distance given for speeds of 53 and 47.5 mph because the extended initial straight line direction would take the ball far out of court.

The figures in the pair of lines titled "SKIM NT IN COURT" (for "skim net, land in court") indicate the distance of the landing point measured inward from the service line under the condition of the ball just barely clearing the net while travelling a "real" trajectory. Notice that the only ball that would go long would be the one hit at a speed of 110 mph from a height of 7 feet, and it would be out by only 5.5 inches.

It must be kept in mind that the figures in the table apply only under the assumed condition of no effects from either spin or air friction. With any decent amount of topspin under real conditions the drops could easily be more than doubled. So the initial direction would have to be adjusted considerably more upward at all speeds to be able to have the ball just clear the net. The slowing of the ball due to air friction has a similar but much smaller effect by increasing the time interval over which gravity can act.

The figures given in the two lines designated "RL PT ABOVE NT" (real point above the net) have special significance. They represent the "window" through which the bottom of a ball can pass and go on to touch ground within the service court. If the bottom of the ball passes over the net at the clearances indicated it will land on the service line. With topspin on the ball the "windows" could be very much greater.

If the clearance is less the ball will touch ground closer to the net. The closest it can get as measured forward from the service line is given in the set of lines "SKIM NT IN CRT" (skim net, land in court). Notice, however, that if a ball with a speed of 110 mph is hit from a height of 7 feet then the bottom of the ball would have to pass 6 tenths of an inch below the top of the net to land on the service line. And if the ball barely skimmed over the net at 110 mph it would land 5.5 inches past the service line.

A server does not need to know even an approximation of any clearance, drop, direction, or landing point as given by the data in the above table, but must not operate with misconceptions about such things as straight line paths, aiming points inside the service court, or the need to skim the net either. Otherwise it is likely that the straight line aim will be directed at a point barely above the net or, even worse, at a spot in the service court. These are mistakes that are very common in spite of being very wrong. If such a straight line aim is at all accurate the ball will land in the net, and that also is very common.

Serving into the sun need not be a problem in recreational tennis. A solution seen in New York's Central Park neatly takes care of it. The side that wins the toss wins the right not only to serve but also to do so looking away from the sun. After the first game the players change courts normally and the opposition serves under the same beneficial conditions, but for two games instead of only one. There is then a change of courts and the special two game service sequence is repeated, etc.

As long as everybody holds serve each side is alternately one game down and then one game up. The end result is entirely normal since neither side can win the set without breaking the opponent's service at least once. This system actually seems more balanced than the conventional since with the latter there is a psychological advantage for the side that serves first of always going one up when holding serve.

The method should not really be needed in expert level tennis because the serve is the one stroke where it is not necessary to be paying more than cursory attention to the ball. The swing is nearly ideal, the hitting point is predetermined, and the ball is automatically made to appear there at the right time. So most of the attention can be directed elsewhere.

chapter twenty
perspectives & expectations

Tennis lessons concerning the basics seem to work best for young children, partly because their days are filled with a great deal of athletic activity, resulting in a rapid development of skills in hitting, coordination, and timing. A young novice at tennis will almost surely be concentrating more on the fun of giving the ball a real whack than on whether it goes in or out. When they are made to pay attention to such things as form, footwork, and consistency many can be expected to lose interest because then the purpose of the game conflicts with their own, which is just having fun.

Adult novices have just as much need of the basics as the children, but adults apply the information on the rational rather than the fun level. And they are not likely to be engaged in day long sports and play activities to supplement the weekly tennis lesson in providing a broad background in athletic knowledge and skills. They are very seldom even aware of any need for such supplemental activity, and have implicit faith that tennis lessons can cover every skill or detail that it is necessary for them to master or know.

Most adults are thinking only in terms of such things as following instructions, emulating patterns, and get-

221

ting the ball to land in court. They defer enjoyment of the game, or the fun of giving the ball a real whack, until such time in the future when they firmly expect to have mastered expert level shots. Although deferring pleasure until the basics are mastered is not a bad idea, it just so happens in the case of tennis that there is a correlation between fun and good technique, between a skillful whack and the principles of hitting, and between unpleasant feel and poor technique.

An important characteristic of good tennis is pleasure. So it frequently helps to play as if hitting is fun, and then it sometimes will be or will come to be. The choice for the student is somewhat between "hit in a way that feels great and win matches" or "stay with methods that are unpleasant and lose." It follows that even if a person elects to disregard all other considerations in favor of the practical reward of winning, that rather short-sighted objective will be best accomplished if the techniques being used have the most pleasant and satisfying feel. Expedients hold few rewards, immediate or eventual.

Attempting to make a shot feel more pleasant amounts to gradually devising the whole set of whatever concepts are required to obtain the better shot. As the effective techniques get to be the most satisfying they will begin to dominate, and the unsatisfying will be compelled to fade away correspondingly.

Required changes in existing details will then be generated largely automatically, rather than that desirable new features will be rejected because of incompatibility with the current package of expedients, or because there will be something about the better methods that the player actually dislikes.

The use of bad tennis habits will not often be deterred solely by the unpleasant characteristics of poor hits: jarring, tiring, off center, jerky, hurried, pushed, cramped, hesitant, violent, deficient in racquet momentum, roundhouse, lacking naturalness, plagued with extraneous motions, hit too early or too late, hit with arm alone, body out of sync with the arm, accidental racquet attitude, etc.

The person with the more valid understandings should be able to devise the better patterns because the effectiveness of a hit is based strictly on physical principles and cause and effect. So the student should have an acquaintance with, or an intuitive feel for, the ideas developed in the chapters on elasticity, reinforcement, racquet attitude, wrist flex, timing, etc. But what is assumed to be valid theory has to ultimately have confirmation in satisfactory feel, otherwise interpretation of the theory could be wrong, or the theories themselves suspect.

A real dependable criterion of the caliber of a shot is not the approximation to a style, or the adequacy for the moment, but the quality of the experience. This is the ultimate guide to improvement because a logical or even scientific analysis of a hit can take into account only the most obvious technical factors. Even for these it is easy to arrive at incorrect conclusions. Witness the one time scientific deduction that it is not really possible for a baseball pitcher to throw a curve, and that what seems to be so is just an illusion.

APPEARANCE vs. FUNCTION

The typical way to teach the fundamentals to novices, as well as to remedy the strokes of experienced players, has been to go through the "basics": grip, footwork, stance, backswing, forward swing, etc. for forehand, backhand, and so on. It works well for beginners, but when used in the attempt to eliminate long time bad habits these methods are of questionable value because they are in effect based on the theory "the function is perfected by means of the style." The assumption is that it is only necessary to mimic an acceptable style and then naturalness, the hit, and elimination of the old habits will take care of themselves.

This is the opposite of what was at one time the battle cry of the modern school of architecture: "form (or style) follows function." In architecture that slogan often led to the sacrifice of elegance and adornment for the sake of honesty, economy, and utility. In tennis, however, the slogan "form follows function" not only appears to make sense and produce results but perhaps, unlike in some architecture, as the function is perfected the most elegant style or appearance may also be achieved.

CAUSES AND EFFECTS

This book has approached the means of improvement by examining the physical principles, mental processes, urges, experiences, and the automatic reflexes that are involved with a hit, and which apply to any stroke standard, special, or expedient in any style. The use of the feel of the hit and the knowledge of the basic principles as guidelines establishes reliable internal standards for evaluating both old and new techniques without bias, as opposed to trying to conform to conventions that are difficult to describe, open to interpretation, and uncertain as to merit.

Improvement is more a matter of recognizing, appreciating, and retaining the good, and thus crowding out the bad, than making direct attempts to discontinue the bad, impose a revision, adopt a new technique, or concentrate on a detail. The intent should be to learn from each shot, good or bad, and to prepare and execute the next shot according to one's best images and understandings of the moment.

The old objectives will always produce the old strokes. To get rid of a bad habit acquired through specific decision (say a deliberate tightening of the grip), or perhaps acquired inadvertently as a compensation for a flaw (say a jerky swing to make up for a late start), the suggested approach involves an examination of experiences and a revision of attitudes and objectives instead of a direct attack on the specific flaw. Removing causes can be successful in removing consequences, but the reverse is hardly ever true.

A CHAIN OF HABITS

A very unfortunate circumstance with flawed games is that there usually is a composite of faults, not a simple basic fault. It is thus not generally possible to eliminate or replace a wrong detail by itself since this amounts to removing a single action from a chain of interrelated actions.

As an example, if a peculiarity in the grip was adopted to compensate for an improper hitting point then changing the subsidiary flaw, the grip, is not apt to have a corrective influence on the controlling flaw, the hitting point. By a similar reasoning, correcting the ostensible basic flaw, the hitting point, is bound to create problems with the left over peculiar grip. But the progressive refinement of the concepts, satisfactions, and the execution of the hit will gradually eliminate both the problem with the hitting point and the related problem with the grip.

Many flaws develop as a necessary compensation for another, and then progress through constant repetition into well established habits that will not quickly disappear in the same chainlike manner of their origin. On the contrary, those that remain will tend to revive those that might seem for a time to have been successfully eliminated. The chain of flaws is thus only as weak as its strongest link.

It is therefore a good idea to have a sequence of priorities. Change a controlling item before a dependant one if the distinction can be determined. Give priority to those changes that seem to promise the biggest improvement, and ignore those mannerisms that are of no consequence to the hit.

LOOKING BACK TO MOVE FORWARD

When that rare perfect shot occurs it may not be easy to recognize what it was that made that stroke exactly right. In any event it is generally beside the point for most people because typically there will not have been sufficient savoring of the experience of the hit, and the manner of execution of the stroke, for them to be aware of even the most exceptional sensations and events. Not recognizing the causes of good experiences is generally synonymous with not benefitting from them either.

Any abnormal swing or unexpected result deserves a moment of reflection about the cause of the variation. If a shot felt like it was not executed properly raise the question as to what went wrong, what caused it, and how it could have been done better. This amounts to just a fleeting visualization that does not detract from concentration on legitimate demands on the attention, or from observation of the actions of the opponent.

While no detail is observed directly and deliberately anything unusual gets registered, and can be analyzed a moment later in a small part of the brief interval before the next shot. The process can be called "retrospective analysis" since the details are recalled to mind without them having been the subject of specific attention during execution. Special attention to details should be limited to evaluation of the experience of the last shot, not to what is occurring in the present or is intended for the next.

When this type of self examination is used the techniques begin to be controlled by educated intent rather than by chance, urges, patterns, habits, and rigid theories. Even when the going gets tough the shots are approached with the idea of producing a great stroke this time rather than with merely a determination not to repeat what turned out to be a disaster in the last.

The suggested approach even has the very important side advantage of taking the mind off wild intentions, emotional urges, lazy evasions and compromises, fears of inadequacy, playing for a lucky shot, resentment of the opponent, anger at a line call, etc.

PRACTICAL EXPECTATIONS

It must be realized that not all shots can provide the same degree of satisfaction, and it is a mistake to expect more than is available. A high soft bounce on the backhand presents such a difficulty to most people. Satisfaction is not absolute but is relative to what is attainable under the circumstances. Demanding more assures disappointments. These in turn lead to a lack of confidence in one's own abilities, and then to the introduction of unworkable expedients. The knack of learning includes an acceptance of the limitations of the situation.

Ordinarily a tennis match is an excuse for reversion to old habits and the occasion for a steady intrusion of new faults. With the approach being prescribed even a tennis match can function as an effective tennis lesson. The game can provide much added interest and incentive if there is noticeable, continual progress, and if a principal objective is to learn under fire what it takes to break away from the current limitations and advance to the next level of skills and satisfactions.

THE ROLE OF DESPERATION

The all-or-nothing attitude that many players have merely guarantees the development and retention of desperation techniques yielding minimal results. Rather than attempting to do the impossible the better trick is to try for a lesser return, which while not winning the point outright once in a big while will not lose it outright most of the time either.

There are times for all players when desperation controls the techniques. This can happen in many situations, from times of real crisis, or when a player reverts back to old fears, to when the expectations are highly over ambitious. It would not be far off to say that desperation techniques are among the greatest problems because of their prevalence and the severity of their effects.

They cause changes in the intents, preparation, position of feet, attitude of body, length of backswing, bend of elbow, reinforcement with the body, timing, amount of push, tensing of uninvolved muscles, etc. In short, just about everything. Since even a minor intrusion of emotion is apt to activate desperation responses it can easily happen that a player's strokes will go completely haywire very suddenly with little instigation.

Examples of the effects on the serve could be that the toss gets to be a trifle off, the body is stiffened as for a great muscular effort, a turn to face the net becomes more pronounced and occurs a little earlier than usual, the elbow is pulled in, the forward jackknife is used, the racquet is pushed forward and then pulled suddenly downward in a pawing motion, and the attention is trained on the target area instead of the business at hand. The odds here are clearly in favor of a double fault, and even if the serve does go in it will likely be highly ineffective.

The presence of desperation controlled responses may be detected just through the normal fleeting visualization at the end of a stroke. If they are found to be present the intents for the next shot should be deliberately switched back to what should be the norm: trying to apply one's best concepts to the preparation and execution of the next stroke, and trying to continually improve on those concepts. Those tasks then occupy the attention, tending to replace whatever it was that caused the previous strokes to go wild.

Do not think of swinging at a hitting point or for an extraordinary result. Think of the larger concept of swinging in a way that gives the shot the best chance of being a good hit. To swing at a hitting point is wrong because that point is a part of the swing, not something external to it. When the hitting point is not considered as being internal to the swing the timing of the external elements gets to be confused with the timing of the internal.

THE CENTER OF CONTROL

There is a great deal of cumulative know-how stored in the conscious mind, the subconscious mind, and the muscular reflexes as a result of the many previous hits and experiences. That part of "know-how," good or bad, that is stored in the reflexes and the subconscious mind is what really constitutes a person's tennis game.

The habits operate so automatically and persistently that it seems that they have been imprinted in a control center for involuntary actions along with such things as blinking and flinching. So whatever is done to appeal to the conscious mind to gain acceptance of a correction will ordinarily not be strong enough to overcome the other more hidden but more powerful controls. A main role of the satisfactions is to overcome the appeal of unwanted habits and thus encourage adoption of the needed changes.

Yet the training and habits resident in the racquet arm do not seem to be transferable to the free arm. When a player injures the racquet arm to the extent of having to learn to play with the other, the swing is apt to be just as clumsy and uncoordinated as when starting from scratch without any previous acquaintance with tennis at all.

LEARN TO LEARN

Each directed experience can expand knowledge and refine the process of learning just as any other skill used in tennis. To the extent that a student blindly imitates patterns, or constantly repeats mistakes, rather than also attempts to discover what is effective and important and what is not, the development of the ability to learn is being neglected. Merely trying again may just amount to reinforcing the problem.

If a stroke is not being improved then it is likely to be deteriorating since there is always a subconscious intent to cut corners and get the desired results without expending the required effort. So when a person's game reaches a peak, and the concepts and the horizons are no longer being expanded, deterioration overtakes and surpasses improvement. Pros are more susceptible than the dubs since they have many more skills to lose, and since they may develop the additional problem of expecting the ball to do more for them than for lesser players.

There are long term consequences to hitting lazy or careless shots because bad habits are very easily acquired. So even at the start of the warm-up it is wrong to just laze the ball back instead of making a special attempt at that time to hit ideal shots. Every stroke during practice should be made with the idea of producing the best satisfactions possible, albeit perhaps not producing the normal pace.

Given the availability of workable methods of obtaining improvement it should be of some sort of comfort to be aware of the existence of remaining personal bad habits, because that only means that one's game has not yet reached its full potential, with many worthwhile changes still being achievable, and with big improvements and more satisfaction as the consequences.

When you are on the court you are alone with your intentions, techniques, the ball, and the situation. You should be concerned only with them. Nobody can do so perfectly, but that is the task, and it should merely be done as well as possible. The rewards are as much in the ideal hit and the learning experience as in the score. It is a game of playing against oneself in an effort to improve one's strokes and satisfactions within the game of trying to win points from the opponent.

Notes on

chapter twenty one
about tennis courts

What has been said of a few of the ideas about tennis strokes can also be said of some of the ideas routinely used in the construction of tennis courts: that not enough consideration has been given to the physical principles involved. The most important penalties for this neglect are poor playability, rapid deterioration, and high hidden cost.

The contracts for the construction of public courts are often necessarily let with more stress on cost than quality. This generally leads to insufficient consideration of the question of usability after the first season. Even the initial fitness for play is apt to be quite poor because some common ideas about useful features and design standards are based on myths not tennis requirements, not even on just the knowledge that comes from careful observation. So public courts excellent in all important respects are very rare.

Once public or school courts are in place they are generally allowed to deteriorate quite badly before money will be spent for extensive repairs. This is understandable in the case of design, material, or settling flaws since the cost of reconstruction is high and budgets are almost always low. The obstacle of the cost makes even minor maintenance a very occasional item for public hard courts. And when it does occur it is usually limited to the patching of cracks, or at most to the spreading of a cosmetic layer of surfacing material over the entire court.

Major flaws will probably remain as long as the courts remain. So the design, foundation, and basic construction better be right on the initial installation. It is therefore well worth the while in terms of preventing the improper design of new tennis courts, and the subsequent many years of aggravation for the users and the ultimate extra costs to the community, to make a thorough study of what constitutes excellence.

The following analysis will relate only to outdoor courts since the indoor are almost always very well built, and since they have no weather problems to contend with.
The major characteristics of good outdoor courts are:

1. A firm foundation so that the court will not settle after being built.
2. The surface laid perfectly flat without any slope in any direction.
3. No irregularities or depressions to affect the bounce or collect and hold water.
4. No edge of the court being lower than the immediately adjacent outside area.

IRREGULARITIES AND LOW AREAS

There are two types of surface irregularities: small dents that cause erratic bounces, and large low areas that can hold many gallons of water. The small are mostly due to poor materials and workmanship, while the large are created by settling and uneven construction. The big puddles that collect in the low areas can cause hard courts to remain unplayable for several days.

When construction costs have to be kept to the economy level there is a tendency to cut corners where it doesn't show initially but where it will turn out to do the most harm: in the foundation. So public courts are notably subject to settling and the problems it causes, which are low areas, gaps between the fences and the court surface, and cracks. These have serious effects on playability, repair costs, and appearance.

Settling can usually be detected by examining the fences and fence posts. The posts are imbedded in a concrete footing placed quite deep in the ground to prevent the fences from being toppled over by winds and frost. When the court itself settles the posts and fences tend to remain in their initial positions. So the first signs of settling of the court itself often consist of gaps between the court surface and the fence, and in marks on the posts or the footings, sometimes in the form of a collar of the surfacing material.

FREE EDGES

An often seen problem is that of an outside area being higher than the adjacent edge of the court. This is especially troublesome when occurring, as it usually does, at the low end or corner of a sloped court. Not only do large puddles develop but a thick layer of gooey mud is gradually built up from the dust that is washed down from the court surface. Sweeping or squeegeeing of the puddles is difficult because of the mud, and because the water can only keep rolling back from the higher outside area instead of being able to drop over an edge and flow away.

A means of mitigating this improper design condition is to dig a slight trough in the ground along the affected edges, something like that on well trimmed lawns but a little bigger. Regular clearing of accumulations is required. If the higher outside area is paved then a possible solution may be a small trough built into the surface just outside the fence. The trough bottom should have a continuous slope so that the water that enters does not just collect and stay there but is made to drain away.

The troughs need be no more than say an inch or two across, and can consist of just two sides sloped down to meet in the middle. This is a suggestion but not a specific recommendation since there may be special needs for particular installations, and since the manufacturers of surfacing materials have not conducted the necessary experimentation to develop reliable standards.

The function of troughs is not to carry away the visible flow that occurs while the rain is still coming down. That flow takes care of itself since water does not pile up but spreads easily and runs off rapidly. The function of the troughs is to drain away the thin slick that remains after the visible flow has stopped. As the film of water at the edges seeps into the trough the rest is spread thinner and is pulled toward and into the trough also. Sometimes the troughs can have the reverse function of diverting water from flowing onto the court from the outside.

Troughs ought not be placed across entryways where people may be caused to stumble, or inside the fences where they can hold both water and tennis balls. In one extreme example seen of the latter the trough was placed directly under the fence, had a rectangular cross section, and was more than deep and wide enough to easily hide a football, or catch and hold barrels of tennis balls.

A slope can be advantageously built into about the last three inches of court surface next to the fences, directed very slightly downward toward the outside. A drop of a quarter of an inch per foot should be sufficient. This facilitates drainage and helps keep balls that land next to the fence from rolling back onto the court too easily.

It is a desirable feature along the outside fences of all hard courts. A trough on the outside is then only required if it is necessary to prevent the water from collecting on the adjacent areas. If the treatment is used along a fence between courts then a slight trough directly under the fence is the natural result. This has advantages but presents a tricky construction problem since the bottom has to have a second slope toward an end of the court, otherwise puddles develop and linger where balls are sure to land.

DRAINAGE ON SLOPED COURTS

An average indoor court, being perfectly flat, radiates a comfortable feel even though the surroundings are comparatively dark and plain in appearance. By contrast, when a person steps onto a typical outdoor court there is usually an immediate and unpleasant awareness of the existence of multiple slopes on the court.

The mistaken purpose of the slopes is typically so that "the courts will be playable within a half an hour after a thunder shower." But playing characteristics have much more importance than draining characteristics. And there are few areas where it rains so often, like for several hours three or more times every week, that it is necessary to install steep enough slopes so that no more than a half an hour of play will be lost after a heavy rain. And strangely enough the slopes create more drainage problems than they alleviate.

It is very difficult to build a consistent slight slope from one end of a court to the other, and the minor variations that are almost sure to occur are apt to result in shallow but sizable depressions. The flat court is much easier to build than the sloped, and is therefore much less likely to be plagued with such low areas.

Slopes do not really enhance water flow to any great extent. If the slant is increased to where it does make a considerable difference then the court becomes very unpleasant to play on, sometimes to the extent of being practically unusable. In installations where flat and sloped courts of the same materials can both be observed under the same conditions it will be seen that the flat courts drain faster than the sloped. This observation can be easily explained by theory.

For example, assume that without evaporation it takes four hours for a thin slick of water to drain off of one half of a particular sloped court. But after those four hours the lower half may be almost as wet as before even though the upper is dry. The reason is that although the film of water on the lower half also drained off within the four hours it was simultaneously being replaced by the water from the upper half. Draining this second accumulation could take another four hours, which means that a total of eight hours could be required.

A similar analysis of the drainage of a flat court reveals that there is a comparative advantage for that arrangement. Let it be assumed that it takes six hours for the water to flow off of one half of a flat court, compared with only four hours for the sloped. But in those six hours both halves of the flat court are drained since each half drains independently to the sides and to the end. There is no upper half to send its load onto the lower half. So under the assumed conditions the flat court would drain in six hours while the sloped court would take eight.

The results for the sloped court could be improved on by installing a steeper slant, and perhaps the time could be reduced enough to equal or better the time for the flat. But increasing the slope to that extent would seriously affect the playability of the court. So then there could be a court that nobody wanted to play on even when dry.

A slope commonly recommended by surfacing material manufacturers is one tenth of an inch per foot of length, but that is almost always exceeded, sometimes considerably. Even a slope of only one tenth of an inch per foot means that one baseline is elevated 7.8 inches above the other. In flat terrain the high end of such a court must be raised above ground level by at least 8 inches, otherwise the lower end will be below ground level and will collect and hold a small lake when it rains.

A device that at first glance seems to offer a complete solution to the drainage problem is to slant the two halves of the court in opposite directions. Each half can drain both fast and independently with this arrangement. But, as might be expected, it raises serious additional problems with playability.

When a ball is hit from one point on such a court and lands on any specific point on the other side, the court surface is in effect an imaginary plane passing through those two points. So when either the hitting point or the landing point changes, the slope of the imaginary connecting plane and the height of the top of the net above that plane change also.

The server is at a particular disadvantage as a result of the net being effectively raised via a double-sloped court. For the server the effective plane of the court extends from the baseline to the service line on the other side, sixty feet away. If the recommended one tenth inch slope is used the height of the net is effectively increased by 2.4 inches above the standard. So the difficulty of getting the ball to land in the service court is increased considerably.

Granular courts (improperly referred to as "clay") have a special drainage problem if sloped, which they almost always are. During a heavy rain the flow of water down the slope carries a fair amount of the surfacing material along too, especially the very small particles. Eventually much of what remains in the high areas needs to be scraped off and discarded because it consists mostly of the heavier particles that look and behave like loose sand. The material in the low spots where the water collects also requires replacement, in this case because the fine particles of which it consists turn into gooey mud when wet.

HITTING UPHILL OR DOWNHILL

When a ball is hit at a specific height either uphill or downhill exactly parallel to the surface of a sloped court the time taken for the ball to hit ground will not vary with either the velocity or the direction, uphill or downhill. As a matter of fact the time will be the same even if the ball is just dropped from the same specific height.

However, the distance travelled will vary with the direction of the hit.

This is so because the acceleration of gravity adds to the component of velocity parallel to the surface of the court in the downhill case, and detracts from that component in the uphill case. So the final velocity and the distance travelled are greater than normal when downhill and less than normal when uphill. The adjustments needed had best be left to instinct since any conscious attention will likely have more ill effects than will result from the initial problem.

The hard court currently used for the main matches at the "U.S. OPEN" tournament has a slope so small as not to be apparent to most spectators. But even that slope has been mentioned by a few tournament players as creating difficulties and requiring compensations in their strokes.

COURT SURFACES

Besides the mentioned four major requirements relating to design and construction (flat, free edges, no irregularities, good foundation) it is necessary to consider the relative advantages of the various surfacing materials as to bounce, friction, comfort under foot, appearance, glare, heat, durability, quickness in drying, reasonable construction costs, and ease of maintenance and repair.

The primary choice is between the granular court and the hard, and the choice is quite easy to make without a detailed examination of all the mentioned factors. If the high cost of a desirable level of daily maintenance and the periodic refurbishing of the granular court can be afforded then granular is the first choice. The avail-

241

ability of water is also an important factor since the granular court should be kept slightly damp.

Almost all recreational players prefer the granular to the hard because of not having as fast a bounce and because of being cooler and softer underfoot. However the bounce off the granular surface is not as true as off the hard. It is in fact comparatively or actually quite erratic unless the court is given a much better than average level of maintenance. Even with good maintenance granular courts tend to cause erratic bounces if the players do not cooperate by continually smoothing the ridges and depressions as they are created during play. Those marks are not removed by standard maintenance techniques, so it is wise to display a sign saying "PLEASE SMOOTH OUT ANY MARKS MADE."

The perfect court has yet to be developed. It should neither be as slick or as uncomfortable as most hard courts, nor like the granular have so much surface friction as to hold on to the ball and give exaggerated importance to spin. It should allow players the same freedom as does the granular to slide the front foot forward and move the body into the hit. The surface material should not shift or dent in normal use. The lines should not be at a different level than the rest of the surface, or have a different friction factor.

OTHER CONSIDERATIONS

Fences are more of a problem than generally recognized. The mesh may have been manufactured with an eye to economizing on materials. So the openings can be large enough that hard hit balls can sometimes go through if curtains are not installed. Another problem is that flimsy meshes may bulge inward at the bottom after a few years of use, allowing balls to roll freely to the outside.

242

The appearance and atmosphere of public tennis courts can be considerably improved, and maintenance costs kept down, by cautioning players against a few unthinking actions. The best way is with signs. An example: "LITTERING SUBJECT TO FINE. THIS INCLUDES CONTAINERS AND COVERS." That notice might well be put up in all public areas. A sign to help minimize refurbishing costs is "DO NOT STRIKE THE NET CORD, NET, OR COURT SURFACE WITH THE RACQUET."

A placard containing a few rules of conduct is also advisable. One that is becoming increasingly necessary is "THE USE OF MUSICAL DEVICES IS NOT PERMITTED." A warning that children not actually playing tennis should be kept off the courts ought also to be one of the items, especially so because tennis balls can be very dangerous. Straying onto adjacent courts can be highly dangerous for anybody, as well as discourteous.

PEOPLING THE COURTS

There is a problem with tennis that doesn't relate to courts, doesn't rate a chapter of its own, is never mentioned in the books, but that ought to be brought up because it is a very important part of the tennis story. And that is the subject of the availability of partners. Many indoor clubs have partially solved this problem for their members with tennis leagues. Players just show up on the scheduled dates and the club assigns the partners, or helps to do so.

On public courts it is almost always just a matter of bringing your own. This means that in most localities there is very little mixing, so regular partners have too many chances to get bored with each other, and newcomers have too little chance of breaking in. Even the regulars are eventually left without suitable opponents, bad enough or good enough as the case may be. The problem gets worse where it is possible to reserve courts in advance because then the matches are all prearranged, and it is of no use for uncommitted players to show up alone at the courts and expect to pick up a match.

A tennis magazine published a report several years ago describing a match arranging system operated via telephone by women volunteers in a large city. The list of registrants quickly went over a thousand. There has been no subsequent mention of the system still being in use, or of the idea spreading. The women obviously had a great idea and initiated a real service, but handling the calls must be a daunting task.

An alternative could be to just set up and announce something like "open tennis hours" to be held several times a week at the public courts in other than prime time periods. This would eliminate the need for phone calls. Players interested in participating would just show up. All matches could be set up on the spot by one or two knowledgeable managers, volunteer or not. The system would probably work best if lessons and prearranged matches were not permitted.

The match arranging system, the suggested alternative "tennis hours," and this book are not really intended to "promote" tennis but just to make better tennis available to those who are committed to the game.

Notes on ===================

Notes on

Notes on ████████████████████

247

Notes on ⊏⊏⊏⊏⊏⊏⊏⊏⊏⊏⊏⊏⊏⊏⊏⊐